T0035708

THE MIDDLE EASTERN COOKBOOK

THE MIDDLE EASTERN COOKBOOK

MARIA KHALIFÉ

Interlink Books

An imprint of Interlink Publishing Group, Inc.
www.interlinkbooks.com

This edition first published in 2016 by

Interlink Books
An imprint of Interlink Publishing Group, Inc.
46 Crosby Street, Northampton, Massachusetts 01060
www.interlinkbooks.com

Text & photography copyright © New Holland Publishers (UK) Ltd., 2007, 2010

All rights reserved. No part of this publication may be reproduced,
stored in a retrieval system, or transmitted in any form or by any
means, electronic, mechanical, photocopying, recording or otherwise
without the prior permission of the publisher.

Library of Congress Cataloging-in-Publication Data available

ISBN 978-1-56656-675-9

3 5 7 9 10 8 6 4

Senior Editor: Corinne Masciocchi
Design: Sue Rose
Photography: Stuart West
Food styling: Stella Murphy
Editorial Direction: Rosemary Wilkinson
Production: Hazel Kirkman
Reproduction by Colourscan Overseas, Singapore
Printed and bound by Times Offset, Malaysia

TEMPERATURE CONVERSION CHART		
Celsius	**Fahrenheit**	**Gas mark**
120°	250°	½
140°	275°	1
150°	300°	2
160°	325°	3
180°	350°	4
190°	375°	5
200°	400°	6
220°	425°	7
230°	450°	8
240°	475°	9

CONTENTS

THE WIDE CULINARY REPERTOIRE and extensive knowledge of Middle Eastern cuisine I possess stem from several sources. I am the editor of a culinary magazine, owner of a cooking school and producer of "Soufra Daimeh," the TV cooking show broadcast both in the Middle East and internationally. During my wide-ranging travels across the Middle East, I explored a passion for cooking alongside local women to discover their culinary secrets, and, through this, improved my understanding of traditional cooking habits. I have translated my experiences into this book, which contains easy-to-follow methods to ensure that cooking these recipes is simple, enjoyable, and exciting.

The hardest part of writing this book was choosing which recipes to include and which to leave out. Ultimately, I decided on a selection that is currently gaining more popularity in Western cultures. I wanted to make sure that while each recipe was simple to prepare, no ingredients were included that could not be easily obtained throughout the world.

Identifying the origin of an individual recipe can be difficult. Many of the finest dishes of Middle-Eastern heritage first emerged centuries ago, and this type of food was often spread by the paths of marching armies over the years, no doubt gaining or losing a herb or two along the way. The Ottoman Turks brought with them the thin filo pastry and the coffee now served throughout the Middle East, while other cultures and peoples also left their marks. The huge diversity includes spices from India, yogurt from Russia, okra from Africa, tomatoes from the Moors of Spain and dumplings from the Mongol invaders. By now, claims as to the origins of a certain dish are varied and hard to prove. For instance, whereas one authority claims the Syrians obtained a certain dish from the Egyptians, another source is convinced it was brought to Egypt at a later date, stolen from the Turks!

Equally important are the produce, traditions, and religion of each country. There is a certain level of similarity between all Arab countries, increasing in strength between neighbors, such as the Lebanon, Syria, and Jordan, or the states of the Gulf region, but each area has its unique culinary characteristics. So, when I attribute a certain dish to one country, it does not necessarily mean that it originated there, only that the given method of preparation is the customary one for that area.

The variety of dishes included in this book reflects the diversity of the Middle Eastern region and the culture and hospitality of its people. Each recipe is given its traditional name alongside an English translation. Ingredients and terms that might be unfamiliar to you are explained in the Glossary (see pages 158–59) and, where appropriate, substitutes for some more unusual ingredients are given.

I have tried to create a balance between using the original preparation methods of the region to preserve the genuine flavors of each dish, and making the process simpler with the aid of conveniences such as a food processor, blender, and meat grinder. If you have the luxury of these kitchen appliances, they will cut your preparation time and make your life a little easier without compromising the taste of the finished product.

Most of the ingredients used in this book will be familiar to the Western reader and are widely available in supermarkets. For others, though, you may have to search further afield in a Middle Eastern food store.

I sincerely hope that you enjoy these recipes, and that this book may help to widen your knowledge and understanding of the rich Middle Eastern culture through its varied cuisine.

Welcome to our table.

STARTERS

Starters, or mezza, are an important part of Middle
Eastern entertaining. It is always a social occasion
when friends and family gather over a drink to nibble
on appetizers and share the latest news before lunch
or dinner. Starters may consist of three or four small
dishes, but an elaborate array of tempting and
mouthwatering appetizers is a more likely scenario.
If you are looking to impress your guests, try the
Parsley and cracked wheat salad (page 10), which
is always received with pleasure. For an appetizer
and a dip, try the Chickpea and tahini dip (page 21)
or the Eggplant and tahini dip (page 13). These are
delicious with barbecued meat or chicken. Starters
such as Spinach pies (page 14), Cheese rolls (page 24),
Meat pies (page 20), and Chicken pies (page 27) can
all be prepared in advance and frozen.

LEBANON

SERVES 4–6

12$^{1}/_{2}$ oz (4 cups) parsley
1 oz ($^{1}/_{3}$ cup) fresh mint leaves
1 small onion, peeled and finely chopped
1 tsp salt
$^{1}/_{4}$ tsp black pepper
4 tbsp fine bulghur (fine cracked wheat)
5 medium firm ripe tomatoes, seeded and
   finely chopped
4 fl oz ($^{1}/_{2}$ cup) lemon juice
4 fl oz ($^{1}/_{2}$ cup) olive oil
Leaves from 1 romaine lettuce heart,
   to garnish

Tabbouleh
Parsley and cracked wheat salad

1 Rinse the parsley and mint thoroughly, then drain in a strainer. In a small bowl, mix the chopped onion with the salt and black pepper and set aside.

2 Rinse the bulghur and drain it in a fine strainer, then transfer it to a large bowl.

3 Remove and discard the thick stalks of parsley and chop it finely. Also chop the mint leaves finely. Add the parsley and mint to the bowl, then add in the tomatoes, seasoned onion, lemon juice, olive oil, and season again to taste if necessary.

4 Transfer to a serving dish and garnish with the lettuce heart leaves. Serve on its own or with broiled or barbecued meat, chicken, or fish.

UNITED ARAB EMIRATES

SERVES 4–6

2 lb 3 oz chicken wings
1 tsp salt
$^{1}/_{2}$ tsp white pepper
4 fl oz ($^{1}/_{2}$ cup) vegetable oil
1 medium onion, peeled and chopped
2 garlic cloves, peeled and crushed
2$^{1}/_{2}$ oz ($^{3}/_{4}$ cup) fresh cilantro,
   finely chopped
2 fl oz ($^{1}/_{4}$ cup) lemon juice

Jawaneh dajaj
Golden chicken wings

1 Rinse the chicken wings and drain. Rub with the salt and pepper.

2 Heat the vegetable oil in a frying pan. Add the chicken wings and fry until golden brown, then remove from the pan and set aside.

3 Add the onions to the frying pan and cook until tender. Add the garlic and cilantro and fry for 3 minutes, stirring regularly.

4 Return the chicken wings to the frying pan and stir in the lemon juice. Simmer over low heat for 5 minutes until most of the juice has evaporated. Serve warm.

Parsley and cracked wheat salad

LEBANON

SERVES 4

1 large eggplant
1 garlic clove, peeled
1 tsp salt
2 oz tahini
2 tbsp yogurt
Juice of 1 lemon
2 sprigs parsley and
  2 tbsp olive oil, to garnish

Baba ghannouj
Eggplant and tahini dip

1 Preheat the oven to 425° F. Pierce the eggplant with a fork. Place it on a baking sheet and bake, or grill over a charcoal fire, for about 30 minutes until soft, turning frequently. Cool under running water.

2 Peel off the skin and remove the stem. Mash the pulp to a purée using a potato masher or a fork.

3 In a small bowl, crush the garlic with the salt and add to the eggplant purée. Stir in the tahini and yogurt. Gradually blend in the lemon juice, mixing well. Pour into small serving dishes and garnish with sprigs of parsley and olive oil.

 IRAN

SERVES 5–6

2 large eggplants
2 fl oz ($^{1}/_{4}$ cup) lemon juice or
  sour grape juice
1 tbsp pomegranate molasses
Pinch of salt
$^{1}/_{4}$ tsp black pepper
1 tsp marjoram
$^{1}/_{2}$ tsp dried mint
2 medium onions, peeled and grated
4 medium tomatoes, peeled and diced

Naaz khaatoon
Eggplants in pomegranate juice

1 Preheat the oven to 425° F. Pierce the eggplants with a fork. Place them on a baking sheet and bake, or grill over a charcoal fire, for about 30 minutes until soft, turning frequently. Cool under running water.

2 Peel off the skin and remove the stems. Mash the pulp to a purée using a potato masher or a fork. Add the lemon juice, pomegranate molasses, salt, and pepper.

3 Transfer the mixture to a pan and cook over low heat for about 10 minutes. Add the marjoram, dried mint, and grated onions. Mix well and cook for another minute, then remove from heat. Mix in the tomatoes and serve hot or cold.

Eggplant and tahini dip

LEBANON

MAKES 30–35 PIES

For the dough
1 1/2 tsp active dry yeast
1 tsp superfine sugar
2 fl oz (1/4 cup) warm water
3 3/8 cups all-purpose flour
4 fl oz (1/2 cup) vegetable oil
1 tsp salt
4 fl oz (1/2 cup) milk
4 fl oz (1/2 cup) water

For the filling
2 lb 3 oz spinach, rinsed and chopped
2 medium onions, peeled and finely chopped
Pinch of salt
3 medium tomatoes, chopped
4 tbsp olive oil
2 tbsp lemon juice
Black pepper, to taste
3 tbsp sumac

Fatayir bi sbanigh
Spinach pies

1 Start by making the dough. In a large bowl, dissolve the yeast and the sugar in the warm water. Stir in the flour, oil, salt, and milk. Add the water gradually and knead for 5 to 6 minutes until the dough is smooth and elastic. Cover the bowl with a damp cloth and set aside in a warm place for at least 1 hour until the dough has doubled in size.

2 In the meantime, make the filling. Squeeze out the excess water from the spinach and place in a large bowl. Add in the onions, salt, tomatoes, olive oil, lemon juice, pepper, and sumac and mix thoroughly.

3 Divide the dough into 3 equal pieces. Roll out each piece on a lightly floured surface to a 1/4-inch thickness, then cut into 4-inch circles. You should be able to cut about 10 circles from each piece of dough.

4 Preheat the oven to 400° F. Place 1 tablespoon of filling in the center of each circle and bring the edges together at three points to form a triangle. Pinch the edges together to seal the pies.

5 Arrange the pies on lightly greased baking sheets. If desired, brush the pies with vegetable oil or beaten egg to give a golden color. Bake for 20 minutes until golden brown. Serve cold.

LEBANON

Hindbeh bi zeit

Dandelion leaves in olive oil

SERVES 4–6

34 fl oz (4^1/$_4$ cups) water
2 lb 3 oz dandelion leaves, rinsed
  and chopped
4 fl oz (^{1}/$_2$ cup) olive oil
5 medium onions, peeled and sliced
  into thin rings
Pinch of salt

1 Bring the water to a boil, then add the dandelion leaves. Cook over medium heat for 10 minutes, then drain.

2 Heat the olive oil in a frying pan, then add the onions and cook until golden brown. Remove half the onions and reserve them for the garnish.

3 Add the dandelion leaves to the frying pan. Simmer over medium heat for 10 to 15 minutes, stirring occasionally until tender and almost dry. Season with salt. Place in a serving dish and garnish with the reserved onions. Serve cold.

LEBANON

Fattoush

Mixed salad

SERVES 4

For the salad
1 pita bread
^{1}/$_2$ romaine lettuce
4 small cucumbers, peeled and sliced
4 radishes, sliced
2 medium tomatoes, diced
4 scallions (with tops), cut into
  small pieces
1^1/$_2$ oz (^{1}/$_2$ cup) parsley, chopped
4 tbsp fresh mint leaves, coarsely chopped
1 green pepper, chopped
4 tbsp purslane leaves
1 tbsp sumac

For the dressing
1 garlic clove, peeled
^{1}/$_2$ tsp salt
3 fl oz (^{1}/$_3$ cup) lemon juice
4 fl oz (^{1}/$_2$ cup) olive oil

1 Start by preparing the salad. Toast the pita bread in the oven until golden brown. Break into small pieces and set aside.

2 Shred the lettuce leaves into small pieces and place them in a large bowl. Mix in the cucumbers, radishes, tomatoes, scallions, parsley, mint, green pepper, purslane leaves, and sumac.

3 To make the dressing, crush the garlic in a small bowl with the salt. Stir in the lemon juice and the olive oil. Just before serving, drizzle the dressing over the salad and add the toasted pieces of pita. Toss gently and serve.

Mixed salad

SAUDI ARABIA

SERVES 4–6

For the dough
1 1/2 tsp active dry yeast
2 fl oz (1/4 cup) warm water
3 3/8 cups all-purpose flour
2 eggs, beaten
3 tbsp vegetable oil
Pinch of salt
1/4 tsp of each: black pepper, cumin, and
  fennel seeds

For the filling
7 oz (1 cup) leeks, rinsed and chopped
12 1/2 oz ground beef
1 medium onion, peeled and finely chopped
2 tsp salt
1 tsp black pepper
4 tbsp tahini
1 tbsp white wine vinegar
4 fl oz (1/2 cup) water
1 garlic clove, peeled and crushed
1 tbsp poppy seeds, to garnish

Aish bel lahm

Bread with meat

1 Start by making the dough. In a large bowl, dissolve the yeast in the warm water. Stir in the flour, eggs, oil, salt, and spices. Add the water gradually and knead for 5 to 6 minutes until the dough is smooth and elastic. Cover the bowl with a damp cloth and set aside in a warm place for at least 1 hour until the dough has doubled in size.

2 In the meantime, make the filling. Place the leeks with the ground beef, onion, salt, and pepper in a saucepan. Cook the mixture over medium heat, stirring regularly until all the liquid has been absorbed. Set aside to cool.

3 In a small bowl, mix the tahini with the vinegar, water, and garlic. Thoroughly mix this into the leek and beef mixture.

4 Preheat the oven to 400° F. Roll out the dough into a circular shape of medium thickness about 12 inches in diameter. Place the dough on a greased baking sheet. Top evenly with the meat mixture and sprinkle with poppy seeds.

5 Bake for 25 to 30 minutes until the pie is golden brown. Serve hot.

SYRIA

MAKES 22 PIES

For the dough
1 1/2 tsp active dry yeast
2 fl oz (1/4 cup) warm water
1 tsp superfine sugar
3 3/8 cups all-purpose flour
4 fl oz (1/2 cup) vegetable oil
1 tsp salt
4 fl oz (1/2 cup) milk
4 fl oz (1/2 cup) water

For the filling
3 tbsp vegetable oil
1 large onion, peeled and chopped
4 tbsp pine nuts
14 oz ground beef
Pinch of salt
1/4 tsp of each: black pepper, cinnamon, and allspice
3 medium tomatoes, chopped
4 fl oz (1/2 cup) yogurt
1 tbsp white wine vinegar
2 tbsp lemon juice

Lahm bil ajine
Meat pies

1 Start by making the dough. In a large bowl, dissolve the yeast in the warm water. Stir in the sugar, flour, vegetable oil, salt, and milk. Add the water gradually and knead for 5 to 6 minutes until the dough is smooth and elastic. Cover the bowl with a damp cloth and set aside in a warm place for at least 1 hour until the dough has doubled in size.

2 In the meantime, make the filling. Heat the vegetable oil in a frying pan. Add the onion and pine nuts and cook until golden brown. Add the ground beef and cook for 5 minutes until all the liquid has evaporated and the beef is brown. Season with the salt and spices, then remove from heat and set aside to cool.

3 Add the tomatoes, yogurt, vinegar, and lemon juice to the meat. Mix well and set aside.

4 Preheat the oven to 400° F. Divide the dough into 2 equal pieces. Roll out each piece on a lightly floured surface to a 1/4-inch thickness. Cut into 4-inch circles. You should be able to cut about 11 circles from each piece of dough.

5 Place 1 level tablespoon of filling in the center of each circle and bring the edges together at four points to form a square. Pinch the edges together to seal the pies.

6 Arrange the pies on lightly greased baking sheets. Bake for 20 minutes until golden brown and serve immediately.

SERVES 4

15 oz (1$\frac{1}{2}$ cups) canned chickpeas
1 garlic clove, peeled and crushed
6 fl oz ($\frac{3}{4}$ cup) water
4 tbsp tahini
4 fl oz ($\frac{1}{2}$ cup) lemon juice
Pinch of salt
Parsley sprigs, $\frac{1}{2}$ tsp paprika, and
  2 tbsp olive oil, to garnish

Hummus bi tahini
Chickpea and tahini dip

1 Reserve 1 teaspoon of chickpeas for the garnish. Using a food processor or blender, process or blend until smooth the remaining chickpeas with the garlic and 2 fl oz ($\frac{1}{4}$ cup) of the water.

2 Dissolve the tahini in the remaining water and lemon juice, then blend with the chickpea mixture. The mixture should be thick and smooth. Season with salt.

3 Pour the mixture into small dishes and garnish with the reserved chickpeas, parsley sprigs, paprika, and olive oil. Serve with pita bread and/or barbecued meat or chicken.

SAUDI ARABIA

MAKES 35 PIES

For the dough
1¹/2 tsp active dry yeast
2 fl oz (¹/4 cup) warm water
3³/8 cups all-purpose flour
2 eggs
1 tsp salt
4 fl oz (¹/2 cup) vegetable oil
1 cup water

For the filling
2 lb 3 oz leeks, rinsed and chopped
2 large onions, peeled and chopped
2 chili peppers, chopped (optional)
Pinch of salt
1 tsp black pepper
1 tbsp corn oil

Samboosak bel-koorat

Leek pies

1 Start by making the dough. In a large bowl, dissolve the yeast in the warm water. Stir in the flour, eggs, salt, and vegetable oil. Add the water gradually and knead for 5 to 6 minutes until the dough is smooth and elastic. Cover the bowl with a damp cloth and set aside in a warm place for at least 1 hour until the dough has doubled in size.

2 In the meantime, make the filling. Mix the leeks with the onions, chili peppers, salt, pepper, and corn oil.

3 Preheat the oven to 400° F. Divide the dough into 3 equal pieces. Roll out each piece on a lightly floured surface into a large rectangle. Brush with a generous amount of corn oil and cut into 2-inch strips. Place 10 strips on top of each other and cut into 1-inch squares. Dip each dough square in flour, then roll out into 4-inch squares.

4 Place 1 tablespoon of leek mixture in the center of each square. Fold ¹/2 inch of each edge over the filling to form a square pie, so that part of the filling is still visible. Press the edges at each corner.

5 Arrange the pies on a lightly greased baking sheet. Bake for 15 to 20 minutes until golden brown. Serve hot.

LEBANON

Salatit al batata
Mashed potato salad

SERVES 5

For the salad
2 lb 3 oz potatoes
2 fl oz (1/4 cup) olive oil
Salt, to taste
1/4 tsp black pepper
1 red pepper, diced
1 green pepper, diced
4 scallions with tops, cut into thin pieces
3 garlic cloves, peeled and crushed
3 tbsp parsley, finely chopped
Juice of 1 lemon
1 cucumber, sliced into rings, few mint
   leaves, and pinch of sumac (optional),
   to garnish

1 Rinse the potatoes. Cook them in salted water until tender, for about 20 to 25 minutes, then drain and peel.

2 In a large bowl, mash the potatoes to a purée. Stir in the olive oil, salt, and pepper. Add the red and green peppers, scallions, garlic, parsley, and lemon juice, and mix thoroughly.

3 Place the potato salad in a serving dish and smooth out the surface with a fork. Garnish with cucumber slices arranged around the sides of the dish, a few mint leaves in the center and sprinkle with sumac, if using.

 LEBANON

Mankoush
Thyme pies

MAKES 6 PIES

For the dough
1 1/2 tsp active dry yeast
1 tsp superfine sugar
2 fl oz (1/4 cup) warm water
3 3/8 cups all-purpose flour
4 fl oz (1/2 cup) vegetable oil
1 tsp salt
1 tbsp dry milk
8 fl oz (1 cup) water

For the topping
1 1/2 oz (1/2 cup) dried thyme mix
   (see page 159)
4 fl oz (1/2 cup) olive oil

1 Start by making the dough. In a large bowl, dissolve the yeast and sugar in the warm water. Stir in the flour, vegetable oil, salt, and dry milk. Add the water gradually and knead for 5 to 6 minutes until the dough is smooth and elastic. Cover the bowl with a damp cloth and set aside in a warm place for at least 1 hour until the dough has doubled in size.

2 Preheat the oven to 400° F. Divide the dough into 6 equal pieces. Roll out each piece on a lightly floured surface into 4-inch circles. Flute the edges of each circle.

3 To make the topping, combine the dried thyme mix with the olive oil. Brush each circle with this mixture and prick with a fork to prevent swelling during baking. Place on a lightly greased baking sheet or griddle and bake for 10 to 15 minutes. Serve hot.

EGYPT

SERVES 5–6

3 medium taro roots
2 fl oz (^{1}/4 cup) vegetable oil
2 medium onions, peeled and thinly sliced
2 tbsp olive oil
34 fl oz (4^1/4 cups) water
9 oz (1^1/8 cup) tahini
4 fl oz (^{1}/2 cup) lemon juice
Pinch of salt
^{1}/4 tsp white pepper
4 fl oz (^{1}/2 cup) water
Chopped parsley, to garnish

Kalkas bi tahini
Taro with tahini

1 Peel the taro roots, then rinse and cut them into medium-sized cubes.

2 Heat the vegetable oil in a frying pan and add the taro roots. Cook for about 10 minutes until light brown on all sides. Remove from the pan and drain on paper towels.

3 Brown the onions in the olive oil. Stir in the taro cubes and cover with the water. Bring to a boil, then reduce the heat. Simmer gently for 20 minutes until tender.

4 In a bowl, blend the tahini with the lemon juice, salt, pepper, and water. Gradually add the liquid to the pan, stirring continuously. Reduce the heat and simmer gently for about 15 minutes until the sauce thickens. Serve cold. Garnish with chopped parsley.

LEBANON

MAKES 24 ROLLS

12^1/2 oz filo pastry
7 oz grated halloumi cheese
7 oz grated feta cheese
3^1/2 oz gruyère cheese
4 tbsp parsley, chopped
1 medium onion, peeled and finely chopped
2 eggs, beaten
8 fl oz (1 cup) vegetable oil

Rkakat bil jibn
Cheese rolls

1 If using frozen filo pastry, defrost thoroughly before use. Cut the pastry into twenty-four 5 x 6-inch strips.

2 Mix together the three cheeses, parsley, and onion. Place 2 tablespoons of the cheese mixture in the center of the shorter side of each filo strip. Fold both left and right sides over the filling, then roll up firmly. Brush the end of the pastry with beaten egg to seal properly.

3 Deep-fry the pies in hot vegetable oil for about 5 minutes, then drain on paper towels. Alternatively, arrange the rolls on a lightly greased oven sheet, brush them with vegetable oil and bake in a preheated oven at 425° F for 20 minutes until golden brown. Serve hot.

Taro with tahini

Sambousik al dajaj

Chicken pies

UNITED ARAB EMIRATES

MAKES 15 PIES

For the dough
1¹/₂ tsp active dry yeast
2 fl oz (¹/₄ cup) warm water
3³/₈ cups all-purpose flour
4 tbsp rice flour or cornstarch
1 tsp salt
3 tbsp butter, melted
1 egg, beaten
6.5 fl oz (³/₄ cup) water

For the filling
3 tbsp vegetable oil
3 oz (1 cup) cabbage, chopped
3 oz (1 cup) green beans, chopped
1 medium onion, peeled and finely chopped
1 green pepper, diced
2 garlic cloves, peeled and crushed
2 chicken breasts, boiled or broiled, and cut
  into small cubes
1 tsp white pepper
1 tsp salt

2 egg yolks, for brushing

1 Start by making the dough. In a large bowl, dissolve the yeast in the warm water. Stir in the flour, the rice flour or cornstarch, salt, melted butter, and beaten egg. Add the water gradually and knead for 5 to 6 minutes until the dough is smooth and elastic. Cover the bowl with a damp cloth and set aside in a warm place for at least 1 hour until the dough has doubled in size.

2 In the meantime, make the filling. Heat the vegetable oil in a pan. Stir-fry the cabbage, green beans, onion, green pepper, and garlic until tender. Add the cooked chicken and season with white pepper and salt. Stir for a few minutes.

3 Preheat the oven to 400° F. Divide the dough into 30 equal pieces. Roll out each piece on a lightly floured surface into 4-inch circles.

4 Place a tablespoon of the filling in the center of each circle. Brush the edges with egg yolk and cover each circle with another circle of dough. Pinch the edges together with a fork to seal. Brush the tops of each circle with egg yolk.

5 Bake for about 20 to 25 minutes until light brown. Arrange in a serving dish and serve hot.

SYRIA ★ ★

SERVES 4–6

8 oz (1^1/$_2$ cups) fine bulghur
  (fine cracked wheat)
1 lb 2 oz lean ground lamb
Pinch of salt
1 small onion, peeled and grated
^{1}/$_2$ tsp black pepper
^{1}/$_2$ tsp allspice
1 tsp chili paste
1 tsp paprika
^{1}/$_2$ tsp dried basil
^{1}/$_2$ tsp dried marjoram
3 tbsp cold water
3 tbsp mint leaves and
  2 tbsp pine nuts, to garnish
Olive oil, to serve

EGYPT

SERVES 4–6

2 lb 3 oz potatoes
8 fl oz (1 cup) vegetable oil,
  for frying
4 garlic cloves, peeled
1 tsp salt
3 oz (1 cup) fresh cilantro, chopped
^{1}/$_2$ tsp dried cilantro
^{1}/$_2$ tsp ground red chili
Juice of 1 lemon

Kibbeh nayye
Raw kibbeh

1 Rinse the bulghur in cold water and leave to drain for 10 minutes.

2 Combine the bulghur with the minced lamb, salt, onion, pepper, allspice, chili paste, paprika, basil, and marjoram. Moisten hands with a little cold water and knead the mixture well to a consistent paste, adding more cold water if necessary. Alternatively, use a food processor and process ingredients very quickly, adding 3 tablespoons cold water.

3 Place in a serving dish and flatten the surface with the back of a spoon. Garnish with the mint leaves and pine nuts and drizzle with olive oil.

Batatos bil kouzbara
Potatoes with cilantro

1 Peel the potatoes, then rinse and cut them into small cubes. Re-rinse and drain.

2 Heat the vegetable oil in a large frying pan and add the cubed potatoes. Cook on a medium heat until golden brown, then drain on paper towels.

3 Crush the garlic with the salt and fry it with the fresh cilantro in the pan in 2 tablespoons vegetable oil. Fry for 3 minutes until brown.

4 Stir in the potatoes, dried cilantro, chili, and lemon juice. Simmer over low heat for 2 to 3 minutes. Remove from heat and serve hot.

Raw kibbeh

VEGETABLES AND GRAINS

Vegetables and grains constitute the main diet of most Middle Eastern people. Eggplants, tomatoes, cracked wheat, fava beans, chickpeas, lentils, and rice are just some of the produce of the land and the flavors of the cuisine.

Vegetables and grains are not only simple to prepare, but are nutritious and a rich source of protein. They are often served as main meals in the form of stews or soups, or ground into pastes, then made into patties. Alternatively, they can be mashed into purées or baked in the oven and served with bread, pickles, or a salad. Their versatility means that they are delicious any time of the day.

LEBANON

SERVES 7

For the pumpkin mixture
2 lb 3 oz pumpkin, peeled and deseeded
2 medium onions, peeled and chopped
1 lb (3 cups) fine bulghur
  (fine cracked wheat)
1/2 cup all-purpose flour
Pinch of salt
1/4 tsp cinnamon
1/4 tsp white pepper
4 tbsp olive oil

For the stuffing
3 medium onions, peeled and chopped
2 tbsp sumac
7 oz (2 cups) Swiss chard, chopped
Salt, to taste
White pepper, to taste
1/4 tsp cinnamon
Pinch of saffron
3 tbsp olive oil
5 oz (1/2 cup) canned chickpeas
2 oz (1/2 cup) walnuts, coarsely chopped

Kibbet yaktin
Pumpkin with cracked wheat

1 Start by making the pumpkin mixture. Remove the fibers from the pumpkin and dice into medium-sized pieces. Place the pieces in a saucepan, cover with water and bring to a boil. Cook over medium heat until tender, about 25 minutes. Drain and set aside to cool.

2 When cool, squeeze out excess water from the pumpkin pieces. Place them in a food processor with the onions and process to a purée.

3 Rinse the bulghur and squeeze out the excess moisture. Add to the pumpkin with the flour, salt, cinnamon, and pepper. Knead to combine the ingredients.

4 To make the stuffing, rub the onions with sumac and place in a bowl. Add the Swiss chard, salt, pepper, cinnamon, saffron, olive oil, chickpeas, and walnuts and mix well.

5 Preheat the oven to 425° F. Grease a 12-inch round oven-proof dish with olive oil. Knead the pumpkin mixture again until smooth and divide it into two equal portions. Place the first half in the bottom of the dish and press with your hands to form a smooth layer. Spread the stuffing evenly over this layer.

6 Divide the second half of the pumpkin mixture into 5 equal portions. Press each piece with your hands to form 3/4-inch-thick shapes. Place the pieces over the stuffing and spread them evenly into a single layer to cover the stuffing completely. Brush the surface with olive oil, then make deep diagonal and horizontal cuts across the surface. Bake for 20 minutes. Serve cold.

LEBANON

SERVES 6

1 lb 2 oz (2¹/₂ cups) long-grain rice
1 tsp salt
3¹/₂ fl oz (scant ¹/₂ cup) olive oil
2 large onions, peeled and chopped
1 lb 2 oz green fava beans, shelled
34 fl oz (4¹/₄ cups) water
Salt, to taste
¹/₄ tsp allspice
¹/₄ tsp black pepper

Foul akhdar bil rouz

Green fava beans with rice

1 Rinse the rice, then soak it in warm water with the salt for 45 minutes. Drain.

2 Heat the olive oil in a large saucepan and add the onions. Fry until light brown, then stir in the fava beans. Cook over medium heat for about 5 minutes. Add the water and bring to a boil, then reduce the heat. Cover and simmer gently until tender, about 15 minutes.

3 Add the rice to the saucepan and bring to a boil again, stirring once or twice, then reduce the heat. Cover and simmer gently until all the liquid has been absorbed and the rice is tender. Season with salt, allspice, and pepper and remove from heat. Transfer to a serving dish and serve hot or cold.

 YEMEN

SERVES 4–6

2 tbsp vegetable oil
2 large onions, peeled and finely chopped
2 garlic cloves, peeled and crushed
3 medium tomatoes, peeled and chopped
¹/₂ tsp of each: black pepper, cumin, cinnamon, cloves, and cardamom
1 whole green chili
1 tbsp tomato paste
5¹/₄ cups water
1 chicken stock cube
7 oz (1 cup) black-eyed peas
4 tbsp fresh cilantro, chopped

Loubia mjafafi

Black-eyed pea stew

1 Heat the vegetable oil in a large pan. Add the onions and garlic and fry for 4 to 5 minutes over medium heat until golden brown.

2 Add the tomatoes, all the spices, the green chili, and tomato paste and cook over medium heat for 3 to 4 minutes. Add the water, stock cube, and black-eyed peas and bring to a boil. Simmer over low heat for 40 minutes or until beans are cooked. Remove from heat and add the cilantro and season to taste. Serve with boiled rice.

Green fava beans with rice

SYRIA

SERVES 6

1 lb 2 oz (2$^{1}/_{2}$ cups) dry chickpeas
$^{3}/_{4}$ tsp baking soda
4 garlic cloves, peeled and crushed
1 tsp salt
1 tbsp dried mint
1 tbsp butter
5$^{1}/_{4}$ cups plain yogurt
1$^{1}/_{2}$ pita bread pockets, toasted and broken
  into small pieces
$^{1}/_{4}$ tsp paprika
4 tbsp toasted pine nuts

Fattit al hommus

Chickpeas in yogurt sauce

1 Soak the chickpeas in water and baking soda overnight. The next day, thoroughly rinse the chickpeas and place them in a large pan or pressure cooker. Cover with water and bring to a boil. Reduce the heat and simmer over medium heat for about 30 minutes to 1 hour, until tender. Reserve 2 fl oz ($^{1}/_{4}$ cup) cooking liquid, then drain. Keep warm.

2 Mix the crushed garlic with the salt and dried mint. Fry in butter for about 3 to 5 minutes until lightly browned. Remove from the heat and transfer to a bowl. Strain the yogurt and mix it into the fried garlic.

3 Place the toasted bread in a large serving dish. Add the cooked chickpeas with the reserved cooking liquid and top with the yogurt. Sprinkle with dried mint, paprika, and pine nuts. Serve immediately.

JORDAN

SERVES 4

3 tbsp olive oil
3 green peppers, cut into long strips
1 small chili pepper, diced (optional)
3 garlic cloves, peeled and crushed
3 medium tomatoes, chopped
Salt and black pepper, to taste
1 tbsp ground coriander (optional)

Shakshoukeh

Green peppers with tomatoes

1 Heat the olive oil in a pan and add the green peppers, chili pepper, and garlic. Fry for 3 minutes until tender. Stir in the tomatoes, salt, pepper, and ground coriander, if using. Cover and simmer over low heat for 5 to 7 minutes until most of the juice has evaporated. Serve cold.

Chickpeas in yogurt sauce

EGYPT

MAKES 45 PATTIES

For the patties
8 oz (1 cup) dry shelled fava beans,
  soaked overnight
8 oz (1 cup) dry chickpeas, soaked overnight
4 tbsp parsley, roughly chopped
4 tbsp mint, roughly chopped
4 tbsp fresh cilantro, roughly chopped
1 medium onion, peeled and chopped
2 garlic cloves, peeled and crushed
1 tsp dried cilantro
1 tsp cumin
$^1/_2$ tsp turmeric
$^1/_2$ tsp cayenne
2 tsp salt
1 tsp baking soda
Vegetable oil for deep-frying

For the dip
4 fl oz ($^1/_2$ cup) tahini
4 fl oz ($^1/_2$ cup) lemon juice
8 fl oz (1 cup) water
1 tsp salt

Pickles and pita bread, to serve
Parsley sprigs and mint, to garnish

Falafel
Fried chickpea patties

1 Start by making the patties. Drain the fava beans and chickpeas and place in a food processor with the parsley, mint, fresh cilantro, onion, garlic, all the spices, and salt. Process to a firm paste. Transfer to a mixing bowl and add the baking soda. Knead to combine thoroughly and leave to rest for 1 hour.

2 Heat the vegetable oil in a heavy frying pan. When the paste has rested, knead it again with your hands and shape it into walnut-sized balls, then flatten slightly. Gently lower the patties into the hot oil, a few at a time, and deep-fry for about 5 to 6 minutes.

3 Remove the patties from the oil and drain them on paper towels. Repeat with remaining patties.

4 To make the tahini dip, mix all the dip ingredients together in a small bowl. Serve the falafel either hot or cold with the tahini dip, along with some pickles and pita bread. Garnish with snipped parsley and mint.

LEBANON

SERVES 3–4

1 lb 2 oz vine leaves
1 medium potato, peeled and cut into
 thick slices
1 medium onion, peeled and cut into
 thick rings
1 medium tomato, cut into thick slices

For the stuffing
12^1/$_2$ oz (4 cups) parsley
1 medium onion, peeled and chopped
Salt, to taste
^{1}/$_2$ tsp white pepper
5^1/$_2$ oz (^{3}/$_4$ cup) short-grain rice, rinsed
 and drained
3 medium tomatoes, rinsed and chopped
2 fl oz (^{1}/$_4$ cup) lemon juice
3 fl oz (^{1}/$_3$ cup) olive oil

Warak inab bil zeit
Stuffed vine leaves

1 Remove and discard the vine leave stems. Place the vine leaves in boiling water, remove immediately, then drain.

2 To prepare the stuffing, remove and discard the thick stalks of parsley. Chop the parsley as finely as possible and place it in a large bowl. Rub the onion with the salt and pepper and add to the bowl. Add the rice, tomatoes, lemon juice, and olive oil and toss.

3 Line a deep pan with the potato slices, onion rings, and half the tomato slices. Place a generous tablespoon of stuffing in the center of each vine leaf, on the stem side. Fold the sides of the leaf over the stuffing, then roll up firmly but not too tightly. Repeat with remaining leaves.

4 Pack the rolls flap-side down in the pan. Top with the remaining tomato slices. Add water to cover the rolls, then place a plate on top of the rolls to keep them intact during cooking. Bring to a boil, then reduce the heat and simmer gently for 45 minutes, until the rice is tender. Serve cold.

 LEBANON

SERVES 3–4

2 lb 3 oz green fava beans
4 fl oz (^{1}/$_2$ cup) olive oil
2 large onions, peeled and chopped
Salt, to taste
8 fl oz (1 cup) water
4 garlic cloves, peeled and crushed
3 oz (1 cup) fresh cilantro, chopped
Juice of 1 lemon

Foul bi zeit
Green fava beans in olive oil

1 Rinse the fava beans. Cut off the ends and remove the strings. Cut into medium-sized pieces.

2 Reserve 1 tablespoon olive oil for later use and heat the remaining quantity in a saucepan, then add the onions. Cook over low heat, stirring frequently until tender, for about 10 minutes.

3 Add the fava beans to the onions and cook for about 10 minutes, stirring frequently. Season with salt to taste. Add the water to the pan, then cover and simmer for 20 minutes until the beans are tender.

Stuffed vine leaves

4 In a separate frying pan, fry the garlic and cilantro in reserved olive oil for 2 to 3 minutes until the garlic is golden brown. Add to the fava bean saucepan. Stir in the lemon juice and simmer for an additional 5 minutes. Serve hot or cold.

LEBANON

SERVES 4–6

3 tbsp olive oil
2 medium onions, peeled and chopped
2 garlic cloves, peeled and crushed
2 lb 3 oz fresh green beans, cut into
   medium-sized pieces
$^1/_2$ tsp salt
$^1/_4$ tsp cinnamon
$^1/_2$ tsp black pepper
4 medium tomatoes, chopped
8 fl oz (1 cup) water
2 tbsp fresh lemon juice
Green salad and pita bread, to serve

Loubieh bil banadoora

Green beans in tomato sauce

1 Heat the olive oil in a large frying pan. Add the onions and garlic and cook until tender. Add the green beans and leave to simmer gently for 15 minutes, stirring occasionally. Season with salt, cinnamon, and pepper.

2 Stir in the tomatoes, water, and lemon juice and bring to a boil. Reduce the heat, cover, and simmer for 30 minutes until tender. Adjust the seasoning if necessary. Serve hot or cold with a green salad and pita bread.

 SYRIA

SERVES 6

3 tbsp olive oil
1 large onion, peeled and thinly sliced
2 garlic cloves, peeled and crushed
15 oz (1$^1/_2$ cups) canned chickpeas
2 oz ($^1/_2$ cup) walnuts, coarsely chopped
1 lb 2 oz cabbage, finely chopped
Salt, to taste
$^1/_4$ tsp cinnamon
$^1/_4$ tsp cumin
4 fl oz ($^1/_2$ cup) lemon juice

Makmoura

Cabbage with chickpeas

1 Heat the olive oil in a frying pan, then add the onion. Fry over moderate heat for 5 minutes until tender. Add the garlic, stirring for 3 minutes, then add the chickpeas and walnuts, and cook for a further 5 minutes.

2 Stir in the cabbage. Cover and cook for 10 to 12 minutes until the cabbage is tender. Season with salt, cinnamon, and cumin. Finally, stir in the lemon juice. Serve hot or cold.

SYRIA

SERVES 4–5

5 1/2 oz (1 cup) fine bulghur
 (fine cracked wheat)
1/3 cup all-purpose flour
1 tsp salt
4 scallions with tops, chopped
4 tbsp mint, chopped
4 tbsp parsley, chopped
14 oz (2 cups) lentils
4 garlic cloves, peeled and crushed
3 tbsp olive oil
3 tbsp pomegranate molasses,
 or juice of 3 lemons

Kibbeh hili
Vegetarian kibbeh

1 Mix the bulghur, flour, 1/2 teaspoon salt, scallions, mint, and parsley in a bowl. Add enough water and knead with wet hands to a firm dough. Roll the dough into firmly packed balls the size of large cherries and set aside.

2 Place the lentils in a pot, add 8 1/2 cups water, and bring to a boil for 20 minutes. Add the remaining salt, reduce the heat, and simmer for about 15 minutes until tender.

3 Add the dough balls, garlic, and olive oil to the pot. Simmer for a further 15 minutes until the balls are tender. Stir in the pomegranate molasses or lemon juice. Serve hot.

 BAHRAIN

SERVES 4

4 tbsp olive oil
2 medium onions, peeled and sliced
3 garlic cloves, peeled and crushed
1 large carrot, peeled and cut into thick slices
2 large zucchinis, cut into thick slices
1 eggplant, cubed
2 turnips, cubed
1/2 small cauliflower, divided into florets
1 medium potato, cubed
3 1/2 oz pumpkin, cubed
3 1/2 oz green beans, cut into small pieces
7 oz spinach, chopped
1 tsp paprika
1 tsp turmeric
1 tsp dried lime or lemon peel
Salt and black pepper, to taste
15 oz (1 1/2 cups) canned chickpeas (optional)
2 medium tomatoes, quartered
8 fl oz (1 cup) hot water or chicken stock

Salona al khidar
Vegetable stew

1 Heat the olive oil in a heavy saucepan. Add the onions and garlic and fry for 2 minutes. Add all the other vegetables (minus the chickpeas and tomatoes) and spices. Mix together, cover, and simmer over low heat for 40 minutes until all vegetables are tender. Stir frequently.

2 Add the chickpeas, chopped tomatoes, and water or chicken stock. Bring to a boil, then reduce the heat. Simmer for 10 to 15 minutes. Serve hot with boiled rice.

SAUDI ARABIA

MAKES 45 PIECES

For the kibbeh paste
2 lb 3 oz potatoes
1 lb 10 oz (5 cups) fine bulghur
  (fine cracked wheat)
Pinch of salt
$^1/_2$ tsp marjoram
$^1/_2$ tsp black pepper
1 cup all-purpose flour
8 fl oz (1 cup) vegetable oil, for frying

For the filling
5$^1/_2$ oz black and green olives,
  pitted and chopped
2 oz ($^1/_2$ cup) walnuts, coarsely chopped
4 garlic cloves, peeled and crushed
2 tbsp olive oil
1 tsp sumac
$^1/_2$ tsp marjoram
$^1/_4$ tsp ground hot pepper

Kibbeh al batatos
Potato cakes

1 Start by making the kibbeh paste. Boil the potatoes until tender, then peel and mash them to a purée and set aside.

2 Thoroughly rinse the bulghur. Place in a bowl, cover with water, and leave to soak for 5 minutes. Drain, then squeeze to remove as much water as possible. Combine the bulghur with the puréed potatoes, salt, marjoram, pepper, and flour until well blended, and set aside.

3 To make the filling, rinse the black and green olives to remove some of the salt. Place them in a small bowl. Add the walnuts, garlic, olive oil, sumac, and marjoram.

4 Shape the potato and bulghur mixture into balls the size of small eggs. Hollow out the center of each ball using your finger. Work your finger around the hole until you have a thin oval shell. Fill the shell with 1 tablespoon of filling, then pinch the opening with damp fingers to close and shape into ovals. Place in a large tray. Repeat until all the filling is finished.

5 Heat the oil in a pan. Deep-fry the balls in small batches until browned on all sides, about 7 to 10 minutes. Remove them from the oil and drain. Serve warm.

BAHRAIN

SERVES 5–6

$^1/_2$ tsp saffron threads
3 tbsp rose water
$^3/_4$ cup superfine sugar
10$^1/_2$ cups water
1 lb 2 oz (2$^1/_2$ cups) basmati or
  long-grain rice
3 tbsp butter
$^1/_4$ tsp ground cardamom
Fried fish, to serve

Muhammar
Golden rice

1 Soak the saffron in the rose water and set aside.

2 Place the sugar in a pan and heat over medium heat until melted and golden brown. Add the water and bring to a boil. Stir in the rice and bring to a boil again. Cook uncovered for 10 minutes until the rice is half cooked, then drain.

3 In a separate pan, heat the butter, then add the cooked rice. Pour in the saffron-rose water and add the cardamom. Cover and simmer very gently for 25 to 30 minutes until tender. Serve with fried fish.

 LEBANON

SERVES 4–6

14 oz (2 cups) lentils
5$^1/_4$ cups water
4 fl oz ($^1/_2$ cup) olive oil
2 large onions, peeled and thinly sliced
7 oz (1$^1/_3$ cups) coarse bulghur
  (coarse cracked wheat)
Salt, to taste
Pickles and salad, to serve

Mjadra
Lentils with cracked wheat

1 Rinse the lentils and place them in a saucepan with the water and bring to a boil. Reduce the heat, cover, and simmer over low heat for 30 minutes.

2 In the meantime, heat the olive oil in a frying pan and fry the onions over moderate heat for about 10 minutes, until dark brown. Add 8 fl oz (1 cup) of water to the pan. Simmer over moderate heat for about 10 minutes, until tender, then remove from heat. Crush the onions with a fork and add them with the oil from the pan to the saucepan of lentils.

3 Thoroughly rinse the bulghur and add it to the lentils. Cover and simmer gently for about 15 minutes until most of the water is absorbed and the lentils and bulghur are tender. Add more hot water if necessary.

4 Transfer to a serving dish. Serve hot or cold with pickles and salad.

Golden rice

JORDAN

SERVES 5

7 oz (1 cup) dry chickpeas
$^1/_2$ tsp baking soda
3 large eggplants
4 fl oz ($^1/_2$ cup) olive oil
1 lb 10 oz tomatoes
9 fl oz ($1^1/_8$ cups) vegetable oil
12 small onions, peeled and left whole
5 garlic cloves, peeled and crushed
2 tbsp tomato paste
16 fl oz (2 cups) water
Salt and white pepper, to taste

Moussaka'a bi zeit

Cooked eggplant

1 Rinse the chickpeas, cover with water, add the baking soda and soak overnight. The next day, thoroughly rinse the chickpeas. Place them in a saucepan or pressure cooker, cover with water, and bring to a boil. Then turn down the heat and simmer until tender, between 30 minutes to 1 hour.

2 Peel the eggplants, slice them lengthways, and season them with salt. Heat the olive oil in a frying pan and fry the eggplant slices until brown on both sides. Drain on paper towels.

3 Cut half the tomatoes into cubes and the other half into slices. Heat the olive oil in a frying pan and fry the onions and garlic until tender. Add the cubed tomatoes and chickpeas and cook for 5 minutes over medium heat.

4 Preheat the oven to 350° F. Place the eggplant slices in an 11 x 13-inch oven-proof dish, add the onion and chickpea mixture, and top with tomato slices.

5 Dissolve the tomato paste in the water and pour evenly over the baking dish. Sprinkle with salt and pepper. Bake for 35 minutes. Serve cold.

LEBANON

SERVES 4–6

14 oz (2 cups) lentils
5¹/4 cups water
7 oz (1 cup) short-grain rice
Salt, to taste
4 fl oz (¹/2 cup) olive oil
4 medium onions, peeled and thinly sliced

Mdardara

Lentils with rice

1 Rinse the lentils and place them in a pan with the water. Bring to a boil, then reduce the heat. Cover and simmer for 30 minutes until the lentils are almost tender.

2 Rinse the rice and add it to the lentils with the salt. Simmer over low heat for about 15 minutes.

3 In the meantime, heat the olive oil in a frying pan and fry the onions over moderate heat until golden brown. Set aside one-third of the onions for garnishing.

4 Add the remaining onion and oil to the pan of lentils. Simmer for 10 minutes until all the liquid is absorbed and the rice and lentils are tender.

5 Transfer to a serving dish and garnish with the reserved browned onions. Serve hot or cold with salad.

EGYPT

SERVES 4–6

2 lb 3 oz canned fava beans
3 garlic cloves, peeled
¹/2 tsp salt
Juice of 2 lemons
3 tbsp olive oil
Pinch of cumin
2 tbsp chopped parsley and
   1 medium chopped tomato, to garnish
Bread, to serve

Foul medammas

Simmered fava beans

1 Place the fava beans with their liquid in a pot and bring to a boil. Reduce the heat and simmer for 5 minutes, then remove from heat.

2 In a bowl, crush the garlic with the salt. Mix in the lemon juice, olive oil, and cumin. Add this mixture to the beans.

3 Transfer the beans to a serving dish. Garnish with chopped parsley and tomato. Serve warm or cold with bread.

Lentils with rice

MEAT

Popular Middle Eastern meats include beef, lamb, and goat. Pork is rarely used because it is forbidden by religion.

The following pages are filled with sensational recipes that are perfect for any occasion. Tender and flavorsome lamb is king of the table. It can be braised, roasted whole, layered with dough, cooked with yogurt or milk, or combined with vegetables and grains. Cut it into chunks or strips, or mince it with parsley and spices to make delicious Kofta (page 70) or Spiced baked steaks (page 72).

Kibbeh, or Ground baked meat with cracked wheat (page 54), the national dish of the Lebanon, is definitely one to try. Whatever your choice, always use the best cuts and never compromise on quality.

LEBANON

SERVES 4

For the stuffing
2 medium onions, peeled and finely chopped
2 tbsp vegetable oil
2 oz ($1/3$ cup) pine nuts
9 oz beef or lamb, coarsely ground
$1/2$ tsp of each: salt, black pepper, allspice, and cinnamon
1 tsp sumac (optional)

For the meat mixture
1 lb 2 oz extra lean beef or lamb, from the leg
1 medium onion, peeled and finely chopped
1 tsp salt
$1/2$ tsp of each: allspice, black pepper, and cinnamon
1 tsp marjoram (optional)
$10^1/2$ oz (2 cups) fine bulghur (fine cracked wheat), washed and drained
4 crushed ice cubes
3 tbsp butter, for greasing
4 fl oz ($1/2$ cup) olive or corn oil
Green salad, to serve

Kibbeh bel saynieh
Baked ground meat with cracked wheat

1 Start by making the stuffing. Fry the onions in the vegetable oil until tender. Add the pine nuts and fry gently until golden brown. Add the meat and cook until all the juices have evaporated and the meat begins to brown. Season with salt and all the spices. Remove the stuffing from the heat and set aside until needed.

2 To make the meat mixture, trim all the fat and fine skin from the meat, then cut into small pieces. Place half the meat in a food processor and process until paste-like in consistency. Transfer to a large bowl, process the remaining meat in the same manner, then transfer this second batch to the bowl.

3 Process the onion with the salt and add to the meat. Then add in all the spices, the marjoram, if using, and the bulghur, and knead to a smooth paste with wet hands.

4 Transfer the meat mixture to the food processor and process again in four batches, adding a tablespoon of crushed ice each time, until the meat paste reaches a very smooth consistency. Combine again in a bowl and knead well with moistened hands for about 1 minute.

5 Preheat the oven to 400° F. Divide the meat mixture into 2 portions. Brush a 12-inch round baking dish with the butter. Spread half the mixture onto the bottom, smoothing it with wet hands. Top with the stuffing made earlier, spreading it evenly over the bottom. Divide remaining half into 5 pieces. Flatten each piece with wet hands and cover the stuffing with these pieces. Carefully press them out with wet hands to make an even surface.

6 Make deep criss-cross lines on the surface with a sharp knife, then run the knife blade around the sides of the baking dish to keep the kibbeh from sticking to the sides. Make a hole in the center with your forefinger and pour the oil over the top. Bake for 30 minutes. Serve hot with a green salad.

LEBANON

SERVES 6

3 lb 5 oz leg of lamb
1 garlic clove, peeled
Salt, to taste
2 tbsp corn oil
2 tbsp white wine vinegar
1 tbsp oregano
^{1}/2 tsp allspice
^{1}/2 tsp cinnamon
^{1}/2 tsp black pepper
1 stick (^{1}/2 cup) butter
2 carrots, peeled
5 small onions, peeled
2 tbsp all-purpose flour
14 oz (2 cups) long-grain rice
1 large onion, peeled and finely chopped
1 lb 2 oz ground lamb
2 beef stock cubes
2 oz (^{1}/3 cup) pine nuts
2 oz (^{1}/3 cup) blanched almonds
2 oz (^{1}/3 cup) pistachios
Roasted tomatoes, to garnish

Fakhda bil forn

Roast leg of lamb

1 Trim any excess fat from the leg of lamb. In a bowl, pound the garlic with 1 teaspoon salt and brush the lamb with this paste.

2 In a separate bowl, combine the oil, vinegar, oregano, ^{1}/4 teaspoon allspice, cinnamon, and black pepper, and brush the lamb with this mixture. Refrigerate for 2 hours or overnight.

3 Preheat the oven to 375° F. Heat the butter in a large frying pan. Fry the lamb for 5 minutes on each side, then transfer to a baking dish. Cook in the oven for about 1^1/2 to 2 hours until tender and brown. Baste occasionally with the juices in the dish. After 1 hour of cooking, add the whole carrots and small onions. Remove from the oven and keep the leg of lamb in a warm place, reserving the juices.

4 To make the sauce, stir the flour into the juices in the baking dish. Add 16 fl oz (2 cups) water and bring to a boil. Simmer over low heat for 3 minutes. Strain and set aside.

5 Thoroughly rinse the rice and soak in warm water for 30 minutes. In a frying pan, fry the chopped onion in 1 tablespoon butter until golden brown, then stir in the ground lamb and leave over moderate heat until brown. Season with salt and the remaining allspice, cinnamon, and black pepper. Add 32 fl oz (4 cups) water, the beef stock cubes, and rice to the pan. Cover and simmer gently until tender.

6 Brown the nuts in 2 tablespoons corn oil. To serve, pour the rice in a serving platter and arrange sliced lamb pieces on top. Garnish with roasted tomatoes and sprinkle with the nuts. Serve with the sauce.

LEBANON

SERVES 4

Kibbeh kbaibat
Fried kibbeh

For the stuffing

2 medium onions, peeled and chopped
4 tsp vegetable oil
1^1/$_2$ oz (^{1}/$_4$ cup) pine nuts
9 oz beef or lamb, coarsely ground
^{1}/$_2$ tsp of each: salt, black pepper, allspice,
  and ground cinnamon
1 tsp sumac (optional)

For the meat shells

1 lb 2 oz extra lean beef or lamb,
  from the leg
1 medium onion, peeled and finely chopped
1 tsp salt
^{1}/$_2$ tsp each of: allspice, black pepper, and
  cinnamon
10^1/$_2$ oz (2 cups) fine bulghur (fine cracked
  wheat), rinsed and drained
4 crushed ice cubes
1 tsp marjoram (optional)
8 fl oz (1 cup) vegetable oil, for frying
Salad, to serve

1 Start by making the stuffing. Fry the onions in the vegetable oil until tender. Add the pine nuts and fry gently until golden brown. Add the meat and cook until all the juices have evaporated and the meat begins to brown. Season with the salt, black pepper, spices, and sumac, if using. Remove the stuffing from the heat and set aside.

2 To prepare the meat shells, trim all the fat and fine skin from the meat and cut into cubes. Using a food processor, process half the meat to a paste-like consistency, then transfer to a large bowl. Process the remaining meat in the same manner.

3 Process the onion with the salt and add to the meat. Add the spices and bulghur to the mixture and knead to a homogeneous paste with moistened hands. Process again in four batches, adding a tablespoon of crushed ice each time and the marjoram, if using. The kibbeh paste should be very smooth. Combine again in a bowl and knead well with moistened hands for about 1 minute.

4 Divide the meat mixture into 20 to 25 egg-sized portions and roll into balls. Make a hole in the ball using your forefinger. Work your finger around the hole, pressing gently until you have a thin oval shell. Fill the shell with the stuffing, pinch to close and place on a tray.

5 Heat the vegetable oil in a pan until hot. Deep-fry the kibbeh shells in batches until browned on all sides. Lift out with a slotted spoon and drain on paper towels. Serve hot with a salad, or cold as a starter.

JORDAN

SERVES 4–5

3 garlic cloves, peeled crushed
1 tsp salt
2 fl oz (1/4 cup) lemon juice
2 fl oz (1/4 cup) olive oil
2 lb 3 oz lamb from the leg, cubed
1/2 tsp black pepper
1 tsp dried oregano
2 large green peppers, cubed
4 medium tomatoes, cut into wedges
4 large onions, peeled and cut into wedges
Salad and bread, to serve

Shish kebab
Lamb kebabs

1 In a small bowl, pound the garlic with the salt until it forms a soft paste. Stir in the lemon juice and the olive oil. Add the meat cubes, black pepper, and oregano. Toss to coat and marinate in the refrigerator for 2 hours or overnight.

2 Thread the meat onto skewers, alternating with green pepper, tomato, and onion wedges. Grill the kebabs over glowing charcoal for 8 to 10 minutes, turning frequently and brushing with marinade so that all sides are coated. Serve hot with salad and bread.

 LEBANON

SERVES 5

3 large eggplants
12 fl oz (1 1/2 cups) vegetable oil
2 1/2 oz (1/2 cup) pine nuts
1 lb 2 oz ground lamb or beef
Salt and black pepper, to taste
14 oz (2 cups) long-grain rice
2 medium tomatoes, sliced
2 tbsp tomato paste
34 fl oz (4 1/4 cups) hot water

Makloubit batinjan
Upside-down eggplant

1 Cut the eggplants lengthways into 1/2-inch thick slices. Deep-fry in the vegetable oil until golden brown, then drain on paper towels.

2 In a separate pan, fry the pine nuts in 2 tablespoons vegetable oil until golden brown. Add the ground meat and cook until browned, then season to taste.

3 Preheat the oven to 375° F. Rinse the rice several times until the water runs clear, then drain. Place half the quantity of tomato slices in the bottom of a deep 12-inch round oven-proof pan. Arrange half the eggplant slices over the tomatoes. Top with half the meat and half the rice. Repeat with the remaining ingredients.

4 Dissolve the tomato paste in the hot water and add it to the pan. Season to taste. Cover and cook in the oven for 30 minutes, then remove the pan from the oven and cool for 5 minutes. Carefully invert onto a large serving dish. Sprinkle with the pine nuts and serve hot.

Upside-down eggplant

UNITED ARAB EMIRATES

SERVES 20

1 small whole lamb, weighing about 22 lb,
   trimmed and rinsed
1 lemon, halved
Salt, to taste
2 oz (¹/₄ cup) baharat spices
   (see page 158)
2 tsp turmeric
2 tsp saffron threads, pounded and soaked
   in 4 fl oz (¹/₂ cup) rose water
2 lb 3 oz (5 cups) long-grain rice
7 oz (1 cup) ghee or shortening
3 large onions, peeled and finely chopped
2 lb 3 oz minced lamb
5¹/₄ cups water
7 oz (1 cup) blanched almonds
7 oz (1 cup) pine nuts
3¹/₂ oz (¹/₂ cup) pistachio nuts
3¹/₂ oz (¹/₂ cup) raisins

Kouzi
Whole lamb

1 Rub the whole lamb with the lemon halves. Season with salt, half the baharat, and 1 teaspoon turmeric. Put aside. Soak the saffron threads in the rose water for 30 minutes. Rinse the rice under cold running water and drain.

2 In a large pan, melt half the ghee or shortening and add the onions. Fry gently until tender, then add the minced lamb and cook until browned. Add in remaining baharat, turmeric, and rice. Stir for 5 minutes over medium heat, then add the water and bring to a boil, stirring occasionally. Add salt to taste, reduce the heat, then cover and simmer over low heat for 10 minutes.

3 Fry the nuts in 3 tablespoons ghee until golden brown. Add the nuts and raisins to the rice. Sprinkle half the rose water mixture over the rice mixture. Cover the pan and leave off the heat for 20 minutes until the liquid has been absorbed.

4 Preheat the oven to 375° F. Fill the lamb cavity with the rice mixture, then sew up the cavity with string and a thick needle. Truss the lamb by tying the hind shank to the foreshank. Place a large rack in a very large baking dish and arrange the lamb on the rack. Brush the lamb with the remaining ghee. Cover the dish with tin foil, pressing the foil under the edges to seal completely.

5 Bake for 4 to 5 hours, basting occasionally with the juices and the remaining rose water. When the meat becomes very tender, remove the foil and brown the lamb. Transfer the lamb on to a very large platter, remove the string, and spoon the stuffing out on a platter. Serve hot.

JORDAN

Mansaf

Seasoned lamb in yogurt

SERVES 6

2 lb 3 oz lamb chunks from the shoulder
Salt and black pepper, to taste
2 fl oz (1/4 cup) vegetable oil
1 1/2 oz (1/4 cup) pine nuts
3 oz (1/2 cup) blanched almonds
2 medium onions, peeled and chopped
1 1/2 tsp turmeric
1/2 tsp ground allspice
1 tsp cinnamon
34 fl oz (4 1/4 cups) yogurt
1 medium egg
1 tbsp cornstarch
4 slices flat bread or pita bread

1 Place the lamb chunks in a large saucepan and cover with cold water. Slowly bring to a boil, skimming as required. Add salt and black pepper to taste, cover, and simmer gently for 30 minutes.

2 Heat 1 tablespoon vegetable oil in a frying pan and add the pine nuts and almonds. Fry until golden brown, then remove and drain. Discard the oil.

3 Heat another 2 tablespoons vegetable oil in the same frying pan, add the onions and cook gently until tender. Stir in the turmeric, allspice, and cinnamon and cook for 1 minute. Add this mixture to the lamb.

4 Place the yogurt in a bowl. Beat the egg with a fork and blend it into the yogurt. Dissolve the cornstarch in 3 tablespoons cold water. Add to the yogurt mixture with 1 teaspoon salt, stirring well. Pass through a sieve into a heavy saucepan.

5 Place the yogurt mixture over medium heat, stirring constantly with a wooden spoon in the same direction. When it begins to boil, reduce the heat and leave to simmer gently uncovered for 5 minutes until thick, stirring occasionally.

6 After 1 hour of cooking, uncover the lamb saucepan and allow the liquid to evaporate until it half covers the lamb. Add the yogurt mixture, stirring well. Simmer gently until the lamb is tender and the sauce thickens.

7 To serve in the traditional manner, place the bread on a serving platter, cover with cooked rice, then pour the yogurt sauce and meat pieces over the bread. Garnish with the pine nuts and almonds.

JORDAN

SERVES 4–6

1 large cabbage
9 garlic cloves, unpeeled
32 fl oz (4 cups) water
1 beef stock cube
Juice of 1 lemon
Salt, to taste
1 tbsp butter or vegetable oil
3 garlic cloves, peeled and crushed
1 tsp dried mint

For the stuffing
1 lb 2 oz ground beef or lamb
10^1/$_2$ oz (1^1/$_2$ cups) short-grain rice
3 tbsp vegetable oil or butter
1 tsp salt
^{1}/$_4$ tsp of each: allspice, cinnamon, and
 black pepper

Yogurt, to serve

Malfouf mahshi
Stuffed cabbage rolls

1 Start by preparing the cabbage. Carefully remove the cabbage leaves, then rinse and place them in a large pan. Cover the leaves with hot water and bring to a boil for 3 minutes until soft and pliable, then drain. Cut the leaves into halves lengthways to remove the hard stalks. Keep the stalks for later use.

2 To make the stuffing, mix all stuffing ingredients together. Place a quantity of filling the size of a forefinger on the narrow edge of a cabbage leaf. Fold over the sides and roll neatly. Repeat until all the ingredients are used up. Place the cabbage rolls, seam-side down, in layers in a deep pan lined with unused cabbage leaves and stalks. Arrange the unpeeled garlic cloves among the cabbage roll layers.

3 Pour the water over the rolls, add the beef stock cube, lemon juice, and salt to taste. Cover with an inverted dish to prevent the rolls floating and bring to a boil. Reduce the heat and simmer until tender, about 45 to 50 minutes.

4 Heat butter or vegetable oil in a pan. Add the crushed garlic and mint. Fry until golden brown. Pour the garlic mixture over the cabbage rolls and cook for a further 10 minutes. Place the cabbage rolls neatly in a serving dish. Serve hot with yogurt.

 LEBANON

SERVES 5

For the meat
2 lb 3 oz shoulder of lamb
^{1}/$_4$ tsp of each: allspice, cinnamon, and
 black pepper
1^1/$_2$ pints (3 cups) water

Dali'i mahshi
Stuffed lamb shoulder

1 Start by preparing the meat. Cut an opening on one side of the shoulder for stuffing. Rinse the shoulder and pat dry. Rub with all the spices.

2 To make the stuffing, brown the pine nuts in a frying pan in 1 tablespoon butter. Lift and drain. Brown the ground meat in 1 tablespoon butter. Season with the salt and all the spices. Rinse the rice and add to the ground meat.

For the stuffing

2 oz (^{1}/$_3$ cup) pine nuts
3 tbsp butter
9 oz ground beef or lamb
1 tsp salt
^{1}/$_2$ tsp of each: allspice, cinnamon, and
  black pepper
7 oz (1 cup) long-grain rice
1 carrot, peeled
1 celery stick
1 cinnamon stick
1 bay leaf
Salt, to taste

Cook over medium heat for 3 minutes, stirring constantly, then add the browned pine nuts.

3 Fill the opening in the shoulder with this stuffing. Close with the help of string and a thick needle or with bamboo skewers. Place in a pan. Add water to the shoulder and bring to a boil, skimming as necessary. Add the carrot, celery, cinnamon stick, bay leaf, and salt. Reduce the heat and cook for 2 hours until the meat is tender.

4 Preheat the oven to 400° F. Lift the meat from the pan and place it in an oven dish. Brush with butter and brown in the oven on both sides for 1 hour. Place the shoulder on a large platter. Remove the string and cut into large chunks. Serve hot with the stuffing.

IRAQ

SERVES 8–10

For the vegetables
5 red peppers
5 green peppers
15 small eggplants
15 small zucchinis
6 small potatoes
1 lb 2 oz vine leaves
16 fl oz (2 cups) hot water
1 1/2 pints (3 cups) chicken stock
2 tbsp lemon juice

For the stuffing
3 lb 5 oz ground beef or lamb
1 lb 12 oz (4 cups) short-grain rice
3 oz (1 cup) parsley, chopped
3 oz (1 cup) fresh cilantro, chopped
2 medium tomatoes, diced
2 medium onions, finely chopped
3 garlic cloves, peeled and crushed
7 tbsp butter
1/2 tsp of each: black pepper, cumin,
  and allspice
1 tbsp salt

Dolmas
Stuffed vegetables

1 Start by preparing the vegetables. Thoroughly rinse all the vegetables. Cut the tops off the peppers and remove the seeds and white membrane, then rinse and drain. Cut the tops off the potatoes. Cut the stems and tops off the eggplants, and zucchinis. Scoop out the flesh of the potatoes, eggplants, and zucchinis using a special scooping tool or a spoon, leaving 1/4 inch of the flesh. Be careful not to break the shells while scooping. Rinse and drain. Soak the vine leaves in the hot water for 10 minutes. Drain and remove the stems.

2 To make the stuffing, thoroughly combine all the ingredients in a large bowl. Fill the peppers, eggplants, zucchinis, and potato shells with the stuffing. Do not fill the vegetables completely; there should be enough space for the rice to expand.

3 Place an amount of stuffing the size of a finger in the middle of a vine leaf on the stem side. Fold the sides of the vine leaf over the stuffing, then roll it up firmly but not too tightly. Repeat until all the stuffing is finished. Neatly arrange the stuffed vine leaves in a large dish.

4 Place any unused vine leaves in the bottom of a large heavy saucepan. Arrange the stuffed potatoes and peppers upright in the pan. Place the eggplants and zucchinis horizontally on top of the potatoes and peppers and arrange the stuffed vine leaves on top.

5 Pour 4 fl oz (1/2 cup) of the chicken stock, the lemon juice, and water to cover, over the stuffed vegetables. Cover with a plate to keep them in place. Bring to a boil, then reduce the heat. Simmer gently until most of the liquid has been absorbed. Gradually add the remaining chicken stock and simmer gently for 1 1/2 hours. Carefully remove the dolmas from the pan and arrange them in a serving dish. Serve hot.

KUWAIT

SERVES 8

7 oz (1 cup) shelled wheat
4 lb 6 oz lamb shoulder on the bone, cut into
 large chunks
10 cardamom pods
1 cinnamon stick
3 cloves
1 small onion, peeled
1 parsley sprig
1 tsp salt
1 lb 12 oz (4 cups) basmati or long-grain rice
2 tbsp butter
5 medium onions, peeled and finely chopped
$^1/_2$ tsp turmeric
$^1/_4$ tsp ground cardamom
$^1/_4$ tsp black pepper
2 medium tomatoes, chopped
1 tsp saffron threads, soaked in 8 fl oz
 (1 cup) of water

Machbous

Spiced lamb and rice

1 Place the wheat in a heavy saucepan or pressure cooker with $8^1/_2$ cups of cold water. Bring to a boil, then cover and simmer over medium heat for 45 minutes to $1^1/_2$ hours until tender.

2 In the meantime, rinse the meat several times. Place in a large saucepan and cover with water. Bring to a boil, skimming as necessary. Add the cardamom pods, cinnamon stick, clove, whole onion, and parsley sprig. Cover and simmer for 45 minutes. Season with the salt when meat is cooked.

3 Rinse the rice several times until the water runs clear and soak in water for 30 minutes.

4 In a large saucepan, gently fry the onions in butter until tender. Stir in the turmeric and cook for 2 minutes. Add 4 fl oz ($^1/_2$ cup) of water and bring to a boil. Stir in the ground cardamom, black pepper, tomatoes, wheat, and rice and simmer for 10 minutes. Cover the rice and wheat mixture with 24 fl oz (3 cups) of the meat stock. Simmer for 20 minutes, stirring twice during cooking. When cooked, sprinkle with the saffron water. Add the meat and simmer gently for 20 minutes. Transfer to a large serving dish with the meat pieces in the center. Serve warm.

SYRIA

SERVES 6–8

3 large eggplants
8 fl oz (1 cup) vegetable oil
2 oz (^{1}/3 cup) pine nuts
3 medium onions, peeled and chopped
1 lb 2 oz ground beef or lamb
Salt, to taste
^{1}/4 tsp cinnamon
^{1}/2 tsp allspice
^{1}/2 tsp black pepper
2 lb 3 oz tomatoes, peeled and chopped
1 tbsp tomato paste
1^1/2 pints (3 cups) water
2 pita breads, cut into small pieces
4 garlic cloves, peeled and crushed with
  1 tsp salt
16 fl oz (2 cups) yogurt

Fattit al makdous

Meat-stuffed eggplants

1 Rinse the eggplants and remove the stalks and caps. Scoop out the eggplants flesh using a scooping tool or a spoon and leaving about ^{1}/4-inch thickness. Rinse and drain.

2 Heat 1 tablespoon vegetable oil in a frying pan. Add the pine nuts and fry over moderate heat until golden brown. Lift with a slotted spoon. Add half the onion quantity to the same oil and cook until tender. Add the ground meat and stir over moderate heat until the meat juices have evaporated. Season with salt and the spices. Stir in half the fried pine nuts and remove from heat.

3 Stuff the eggplants with the meat mixture, then fry them in 4 tablespoons vegetable oil over moderate heat until lightly browned on all sides. Remove to a plate.

4 To make a tomato sauce, fry the remaining onion in 1 tablespoon vegetable oil until tender. Add the tomatoes and cook over moderate heat for 10 minutes. Stir in the tomato paste and water, season to taste, and bring to a boil. Heat, cover, and cook for 10 minutes.

5 Place the eggplants in the pan with the tomato sauce. Cover and simmer for 15 minutes until tender. Fry the bread pieces in hot vegetable oil until browned, then remove to a plate.

6 In a bowl, mix the garlic and salt with the yogurt. To serve, place the fried bread pieces on a serving dish, top with the eggplants and cover with tomato sauce. Finally, pour the yogurt over the top and sprinkle with pine nuts.

EGYPT

SERVES 5–6

2 lb 3 oz ground beef or lamb
2 medium onions, peeled and chopped
3 oz (1 cup) parsley, chopped
1 tsp ground cinnamon
1 tsp allspice
1/2 tsp black pepper
1/2 tsp cumin (optional)
2 tsp salt
1 tbsp vegetable oil
Pita bread and salad, to serve

Kofta
Ground meat with parsley

1 Place the ground meat, onions, parsley, cinnamon, allspice, black pepper, cumin, if using, and salt in a food processor. Process briefly to a homogeneous paste. Transfer to a bowl, and cover and refrigerate for 2 hours to bring out flavors.

2 Divide the meat mixture into 20 equal portions. Form each portion into fingers about 5 inches long. Thread each finger lengthways on a skewer. Grill over glowing charcoal for about 10 minutes, turning frequently until well done. Remove from the skewers. Serve with pita bread and salad.

SAUDI ARABIA

SERVES 6

2 lb 3 oz lamb, cubed
3 medium onions, peeled and finely chopped
Salt and black pepper, to taste
34 fl oz (4 1/4 cups) water
1/8 tsp cardamom pods
1/8 tsp mastic
16 fl oz (2 cups) milk
14 oz (2 cups) basmati or long-grain rice, rinsed
4 tbsp melted butter
Green salad, to serve

Saliq
Lamb with milk and rice

1 Place the meat, onions, salt, and black pepper in a saucepan. Cover with water and bring to a boil, skimming as necessary. Add the cardamom and mastic. Cover and simmer gently for 1 hour until the meat is tender. Add water if necessary. Remove the meat from the pan and keep warm.

2 Add 16 fl oz (2 cups) water and the milk to the stock in which the meat was cooked and bring to a boil. Stir in the rice, cover, and cook gently over low heat for about 15 minutes, until the rice is just cooked. Turn off the heat and keep covered for 10 minutes to allow to steam. Place the rice on a large serving platter. Arrange the pieces of meat on top. Pour the melted butter over the rice and meat. Serve with a green salad.

Ground meat with parsley

LEBANON

SERVES 4–5

2 lb 3 oz sirloin steak, cut into
  Julienne strips
1/4 tsp ground mastic
1/8 tsp of each: ground cardamom,
  ground cloves, ground nutmeg, allspice,
  and black pepper
1/4 tsp cinnamon
2 bay leaves, shredded into small pieces
1 tsp salt
1 lemon peel
2 fl oz (1/4 cup) lemon juice
2 fl oz (1/4 cup) white wine vinegar
4 fl oz (1/2 cup) vegetable oil
3 garlic cloves, peeled and crushed
2 large onions, peeled and sliced
7 oz finely minced fat (optional)
5 small tomatoes, halved
Pita bread, tahini sauce, snipped parsley,
  onion rings, and pickles, to serve

Shawarma

Spiced baked steaks

1 Place the meat strips in a large bowl. In a small bowl, combine the mastic, cardamom, cloves, nutmeg, allspice, black pepper, cinnamon, bay leaves, and salt. Sprinkle the mixed spices over the meat. Add the lemon peel, lemon juice, vinegar, vegetable oil, garlic, and onions. Mix well. Cover and marinate overnight in the refrigerator.

2 Preheat the oven to 400° F. Place the meat with the marinade in a large baking dish and remove the lemon peel. Add the minced fat if using. Top with the tomatoes. Bake for 30 minutes, until most of the liquid has evaporated, stirring once or twice. Serve with pita bread, tahini sauce, snipped parsley, onion rings, and pickles.

 BAHRAIN

SERVES 4

7 oz (1 cup) lentils
7 oz (1 cup) bulghur (cracked wheat),
  soaked in water and drained
9 oz ground lamb
1 medium onion, peeled and finely chopped
1 1/2 oz (1/2 cup) parsley, chopped
1/2 tsp salt
1/4 tsp black pepper
1 tsp marjoram
5 fresh or dried basil leaves, finely chopped
2 oz (1/3 cup) pine nuts

To garnish
1 red pepper, sliced in rings
1 green pepper, sliced in rings
2 tbsp blanched almonds (optional)

Kibbeh bil adas

Raw meat with cracked wheat and lentils

1 Place the lentils in a saucepan, cover with water and bring to a boil. Cook over moderate heat until tender, then drain. Combine the lentils and the bulghur, then process in a food processor. Set aside.

2 Combine the ground lamb with the onion, parsley, salt, black pepper, marjoram, and basil. Process in a food processor to a consistent paste.

3 Add the pine nuts to the lentils and bulghur mixture and mix thoroughly. Transfer the mixture to a serving dish. Garnish with green and red peppers and sprinkle with almonds, if desired.

Spiced baked steaks

YEMEN

SERVES 4

3 tbsp vegetable oil
2 medium onions, peeled and sliced
1 lb 2 oz beef chuck, cut into large chunks
3 medium tomatoes, chopped
1 large green pepper, sliced
2 garlic cloves, peeled and crushed
1 1/2 pints (3 cups) water
1/2 tbsp hawail spices (see page 158)
2 tbsp fresh cilantro, chopped
2 medium carrots, peeled and grated
Boiled white rice, to serve

Lahm al aqda
Beef with tomato sauce

1 Heat the vegetable oil in a large pan. Add the onions and fry over medium heat for 5 minutes until tender. Add the beef chunks and cook until brown on all sides. Add the tomatoes, green pepper, garlic, water, and hawail spices and bring to a boil, then reduce the heat. Cover and simmer gently for 1 hour, until the meat is tender. Add the cilantro and carrots and cook for a further 5 minutes. Serve hot with boiled white rice.

LEBANON

SERVES 4
2 tbsp corn oil or butter
1 lb 2 oz lamb or beef shanks, cubed
Salt and black pepper, to taste
16 fl oz (2 cups) water
6 large onions, peeled and sliced
4 1/4 cups yogurt
1 tbsp cornstarch
1 medium egg white

Laban immou
Meat in yogurt sauce

1 Heat the corn oil or butter in a saucepan until hot. Add the meat and cook over medium heat until brown on all sides. Season with salt and black pepper to taste. Add the water to the pan and bring to a boil. Cover and simmer over low heat for 30 minutes, skimming as necessary. Add the onions and bring to a boil, then reduce the heat. Cover and simmer for a further 30 minutes until the lamb is tender.

2 Meanwhile, place the yogurt in a bowl and mix with the cornstarch and whisked egg white. Strain through a sieve into a heavy pan. Place the pan over medium heat, stirring constantly in one direction with a wooden spoon until the yogurt starts to boil. Reduce heat and simmer gently, uncovered, for 3 minutes, stirring occasionally.

3 Pour the yogurt over the meat mixture and gently return to a boil. Simmer for 10 minutes and adjust the seasoning if necessary. Serve hot with boiled white rice.

IRAQ

Kibbeh hamoud
Kibbeh with lemon

SERVES 4–6

For the beef shells
14 oz (2 cups) short-grain or regular rice
1 lb 2 oz lean ground beef
3 tbsp parsley, finely chopped
Salt and black pepper, to taste

For the stuffing
9 oz ground beef
1 medium onion, peeled and finely chopped
1 tsp allspice
$^1/_2$ tsp black pepper
Pinch of saffron soaked in 2 tbsp rose water

For the sauce
2 tbsp olive oil
4 garlic cloves, peeled and sliced
4 medium tomatoes, peeled and chopped
2 tbsp tomato paste
Juice of 2 small lemons
34 fl oz (4$^1/_4$ cups) water
Black pepper and dry mint, to taste

Boiled rice, to serve

1 Start by preparing the beef shells. Cover the rice with water and soak for 1$^1/_2$ hours. Drain and process in a food processor until powdery. Add the beef, parsley, salt, and black pepper and process for 3 to 4 minutes until all the ingredients are well combined.

2 To make the stuffing, combine the ground beef with the onion, spices, and saffron water in a bowl and mix well.

3 Divide the beef shell mixture into 20 to 25 egg-sized portions and roll into balls. Make a hole in the ball using your forefinger. Work your finger around the hole pressing gently until you have a thin oval shell of $^1/_4$-inch thickness. Fill the shell with the stuffing, close and press firmly on both ends and place on a tray.

4 To make the sauce, heat the olive oil in a large saucepan and lightly fry the garlic. Add tomatoes, tomato paste, lemon juice, and water and bring to a boil. Gently add the stuffed meat balls one by one. Cover and simmer for 1 hour until well done. Sprinkle with black pepper and dry mint and serve with boiled rice.

IRAQ

SERVES 4–6

12 small lamb shanks
2 medium onions, peeled and finely chopped
2 fl oz (1/4 cup) olive oil
2 garlic cloves, peeled and chopped
1 tsp baharat spices (see page 158)
1/2 tsp turmeric
5 medium tomatoes, peeled and chopped
8 fl oz (1 cup) water
1 tbsp tomato paste
1 bay leaf
1 dried lime or rind of 1 lemon
Salt and black pepper, to taste
Boiled white rice and salad, to serve

Kouzi ala timman
Lamb shanks with tomato sauce and rice

1 Rinse the lamb shanks in cold water, pat dry, and place in an oven-proof dish.

2 In a pan, gently fry the onions in the olive oil until tender. Add the garlic, baharat, and turmeric and fry for 1 minute. Add the remaining ingredients and bring to a boil, then simmer over low heat for 5 minutes.

3 Preheat the oven to 375° F. Pour the tomato sauce over the lamb shanks, cover with tin foil and cook in the oven for 1 1/2 to 2 hours until the meat is very tender and separates easily from the bone. Arrange the shanks on a bed of boiled white rice, pour the sauce on top, and serve with salad.

SAUDI ARABIA

SERVES 5

2 tbsp olive oil
2 large onions, peeled and chopped
2 lb 3 oz boneless stewing lamb
  or beef, trimmed and cubed
2 tsp baharat spices (see page 158)
2 garlic cloves, peeled and crushed
2 medium tomatoes, peeled and chopped
2 tbsp tomato paste
2 tsp salt
1/2 tsp ground black pepper
1 oz (1/3 cup) parsley, chopped
2 lb 3 oz potatoes, peeled
1 flat bread or pita bread
Chopped parsley, to garnish
Pickles, to serve

Tharyd
Meat and potato stew

1 Heat the olive oil in a heavy saucepan. Add the onions and fry over moderate heat until tender. Increase the heat and add the meat cubes, stirring frequently for about 20 minutes until all the liquid has evaporated and the meat is brown on all sides. Add the baharat and garlic and cook for 1 minute.

2 Add the tomatoes, tomato paste, salt, black pepper, and parsley. Cover and simmer over low heat for 1 hour. Halve the potatoes if large. Add to the pan, cover and simmer for about 30 minutes until the meat and potatoes are tender.

3 Cut the bread into small pieces and place on a serving dish. Top with the meat, potatoes, and sauce and sprinkle with chopped parsley. Serve with pickles.

Lamb shanks with tomato sauce and rice

LEBANON

SERVES 5–6

2 lb 3 oz lean ground beef
1 medium onion, peeled and finely chopped
1 tsp salt
1/2 tsp cinnamon
1/2 tsp allspice
4 fl oz (1/2 cup) vegetable oil
2 lb 3 oz small onions, peeled
2 tbsp pomegranate molasses or
  juice of 1 lemon
34 fl oz (4 1/4 cups) water
2 tbsp all-purpose flour
3 garlic cloves, peeled and crushed
1 tsp dried mint
Boiled rice, to serve

Dawood basha
Meatballs with onion

1 Place the meat, onion, salt, and half the spices in food processor. Cover and process briefly to form a homogeneous, firm paste. With wet hands, roll the meat mixture into small walnut-sized balls.

2 Heat the vegetable oil in a frying pan until hot. Cook the meatballs in batches over moderate heat until browned all over. Lift out with a slotted spoon and drain on paper towels.

3 Fry the whole small onions in the same oil until golden brown. Transfer the meatballs and onions to a large saucepan. Add the pomegranate molasses or lemon juice, water, and remaining spices to the pan. Bring to a boil, then cover and simmer over low heat for 30 minutes.

4 Dissolve the flour in 4 fl oz (1/2 cup) cold water. Add to the meat, stirring continuously for 1 minute until the sauce has thickened. Add the garlic and dried mint to the meat and cook for 5 minutes. Serve hot with boiled rice.

SAUDI ARABIA

SERVES 8

4 lb 6 oz leg of lamb
1 1/2 cups yogurt
2 tbsp tomato paste
3 garlic cloves, peeled and chopped
1 tsp of each: black pepper, cardamom,
  cinnamon, and cumin
1 tsp saffron
Salt, to taste
4 fl oz (1/2 cup) corn oil
Cooked vegetables and boiled rice, to serve

Fakhtha bel laban
Leg of lamb with yogurt

1 Trim the leg of lamb and remove the membrane and any excess fat. Slash in several places with a sharp knife.

2 In a bowl, mix the yogurt with the remaining ingredients. Brush the lamb with this mixture and marinate, in the refrigerator, for 3 hours or overnight.

3 Preheat the oven to 375° F. Place the lamb in a large oven-proof dish and cover with tin foil. Keep the marinade for later use. Cook in the oven for 2 to 2 1/2 hours, basting with the marinade two or three times during the final stages of cooking to prevent drying. Slice and serve with cooked vegetables and boiled rice.

EGYPT

Bamia bi salsat al tamatim

Okra in tomato sauce

SERVES 5

2 lb 3 oz okra
2 tbsp ghee or shortening
1 medium onion, peeled and chopped
1 lb 2 oz stewing beef or lamb, cubed
Salt and black pepper, to taste
1 lb 2 oz tomatoes, peeled and chopped
8 fl oz (1 cup) water
1 tbsp tomato paste
3 tbsp vegetable oil
4 garlic cloves, peeled and crushed
1 tbsp dried cilantro
1 green chili, chopped (optional)
Juice of 1 lemon
Boiled white rice, to serve

1 Trim the okra stems, taking care not to cut through flesh and to keep the cap intact. Rinse, drain, and pat dry with paper towels. Set aside.

2 Melt 1 tablespoon of the ghee or shortening in a pan, add the onion and cook over medium heat until tender. Add the meat and brown on all sides. Season with salt and black pepper. Add the tomatoes and cook for about 5 minutes, then stir in the water and the tomato paste. Cover and cook over moderate heat for 45 minutes until the meat is almost cooked.

3 In a separate pan, fry the okra in the vegetable oil over moderate heat until slightly browned. Add the okra to the meat pan, cover, and cook for 20 minutes.

4 Heat the remaining ghee or shortening in a small pan. Add the garlic, cilantro, and chili, if using. Cook, stirring gently until browned. Pour the hot garlic mixture over the okra. Add lemon juice and cook for 10 minutes. Serve hot with boiled white rice.

YEMEN

Hore'i

Spiced beef shanks

SERVES 4

2 lb 3 oz beef shanks with bones, cut into
  thick chunks
2 medium onions, peeled and quartered
5 garlic cloves, peeled
3 medium tomatoes, peeled and chopped
Salt and black pepper, to taste
$1/2$ tsp caraway
$1/4$ tsp of each: saffron threads, cardamom,
  and turmeric
1–2 hot red chili peppers, chopped
Boiled white rice, to serve

1 Place the beef chunks in a large saucepan and cover with cold water. Bring to a boil, skimming as necessary. Add the onions, garlic, tomatoes, salt, black pepper, and spices. Add 1 or 2 chili peppers, as desired. Cover and simmer over low heat for about $1^{1}/2$ hours until the meat is tender and the juice has reduced to a thick sauce. Serve hot with boiled white rice.

CHICKEN

Some of the tastiest Middle Eastern dishes feature chicken. These range from the inspired simplicity of grilled and roasted preparations to the elaborate dishes cooked with rice or walnuts. The simple yet creative ideas for cooking chicken are as limitless as they are tempting.

In the following pages, you will find flavorsome Chicken kebabs (page 84), marinated in exotic spices and grilled on skewers with mushrooms, and the popular Lebanese baked chicken fingers (page 89), marinated in a mixture of garlic, lemon juice, and exotic spices, along with a whole host of delectable chicken dishes. These recipes are sure to make your guests happy and coming back for more.

IRAN

SERVES 5

14 oz (2 cups) basmati or long-grain rice
4 fl oz (^{1}/2 cup) vegetable oil
1 large onion, peeled and chopped
Small whole chicken, rinsed, and cut
  into 4 pieces
16 fl oz (2 cups) hot water
Salt and black pepper, to season
1 cup superfine sugar
^{1}/2 tsp saffron
3 oz (1 cup) orange peel
2 tbsp butter
2^1/2 oz (^{1}/2 cup) slivered almonds, soaked
  in cold water for 1 hour
2^1/2 oz (^{1}/2 cup) slivered pistachios

Shirin polow
Chicken with rice and orange peel

1 Rinse the rice twice and soak in warm water for 1 hour.

2 Heat half the vegetable oil in a pan. Add the onion and fry until slightly browned. Add the chicken pieces and fry until slightly browned. Stir in the hot water, salt, and pepper and bring to a boil. Cook over medium heat for about 20 minutes. Remove the chicken pieces from the pan and remove the bones.

3 Set aside 3 tablespoons sugar for later use. In the same pan, add the remaining sugar to 8 fl oz (1 cup) hot water and bring to a boil. Add 4 fl oz (^{1}/2 cup) chicken stock to the pan with 2 tablespoons oil and the saffron and mix well. Set aside for later use.

4 Thinly slice the orange peel and boil for a few minutes, drain and repeat the process three times. Soak in cold water for 1 hour, then drain. Finally, boil for a few minutes with the reserved sugar and drain.

5 Pour 6^1/4 cups water into a large nonstick pan and bring to a boil. Add the rice and 2 teaspoons salt. Cook until the rice is slightly soft. Drain and rinse in warm water.

6 Pour 1 tablespoon oil and 1 tablespoon butter into the same pan and add half the rice. Pour another tablespoon oil and the remaining butter over the rice, cover the pan and cook over low heat for about 30 minutes. Spread the chicken pieces over the rice, and cover with half of the remaining rice. Spread half the almonds and orange peel over the rice and cover with remaining rice. Pour the sugar and reserved chicken stock over the rice. Cover and cook over low heat for about 30 minutes. Add the remaining almonds, orange peel, and the pistachios and mix well. Transfer to a serving dish and serve immediately.

LEBANON

SERVES 5

2 lb 3 oz chicken breasts, deboned
  and cubed
1 tbsp ketchup
1 tbsp tomato paste
1 tsp salt
$^1/_4$ tsp white pepper
4 garlic cloves, peeled and crushed
4 fl oz ($^1/_2$ cup) lemon juice
4 fl oz ($^1/_2$ cup) vegetable oil
1 tsp oregano
2 green peppers, cubed
7 oz button mushrooms
Pita bread and salad, to serve

Shish tawook
Chicken kebabs

1 Mix all the ingredients together in a bowl. Cover and marinate overnight in the refrigerator.

2 Thread the chicken pieces onto skewers, alternating chicken pieces with cubes of green pepper and whole mushrooms. The above quantities will make about 10 skewers.

3 Grill over glowing charcoal for 10 to 12 minutes, turning frequently and brushing with the marinade when required. Alternatively, place in an oven-proof dish and cook in a preheated oven at 375° F for 30 minutes until tender. Serve with pita bread and salad.

 BAHRAIN

SERVES 4–6

Medium whole chicken, cut into 8 pieces
$6^1/_4$ cups water
3 tbsp vegetable oil
2 medium onions, peeled and finely chopped
2 garlic cloves, peeled and crushed
1 small piece of fresh ginger, peeled and
  crushed
1 tbsp tomato paste
2 large potatoes, peeled and cubed
4 zucchinis, cubed
2 medium eggplants, cubed
3 medium tomatoes, chopped
2 dried limes or 1 lemon rind
1 small hot green chili, chopped
1 tsp baharat spices (see page 158)
$^1/_4$ tsp of each: cinnamon, turmeric, curry
  powder, garlic powder, ground coriander,
  cardamom
Pinch of hot chili powder
1 green pepper, cut into thick slices
3 oz (1 cup) fresh cilantro, chopped
Boiled rice, to serve

Dajaj salona
Chicken with vegetables

1 Place the chicken pieces in a large pan. Add the water and bring to a boil, skimming as necessary. Cover and cook over low heat for 25 minutes. Lift the chicken from pan, strain the stock and reserve.

2 Heat the vegetable oil in a large saucepan. Add the onions and cook until golden brown. Stir in the garlic, ginger, tomato paste, potatoes, zucchinis, eggplants, tomatoes, dried lime or lemon rind, and chili and cook for 5 minutes.

3 Add the chicken pieces to the pan, along with the reserved stock, baharat spices, all the spices, and the green pepper. Bring to a boil, then cover and simmer for 10 minutes. Add the cilantro, and simmer for a further 10 minutes until the potato and chicken are tender. Serve with boiled rice.

Chicken with vegetables

SERVES 4

For the squabs
4 squabs, with giblets reserved
Salt and black pepper, to season
2 cardamom pods, bruised

For the stuffing
5^1/$_2$ oz (^{3}/$_4$ cup) green wheat (freek, see
  page 158), or rice
1 tbsp butter
1 medium onion, peeled and finely chopped
4 garlic cloves, peeled and crushed
4 tbsp fresh cilantro, chopped
2 fl oz (^{1}/$_4$ cup) lemon juice
1 small onion, peeled
Salt and black pepper, to season

Parsley sprigs, to garnish

Hamam mishshi bil freek

Wheat-stuffed squabs

1 Start by preparing the squabs. Rinse and drain them, then season them inside and out with salt and pepper. Clean and finely chop the livers. Cover and refrigerate until required.

2 To make the stuffing, place the green wheat in a bowl and soak in water for 5 minutes. Strain and squeeze the wheat to extract all the liquid. If using rice instead of green wheat, rinse the rice and drain thoroughly. Heat the butter in a frying pan and gently fry the medium onion until tender. Add the chopped livers and fry until browned on both sides. Add the garlic, cilantro, lemon juice, half the small onion, and seasoning. Simmer for 3 minutes, stirring occasionally. Stir in the green wheat or rice and cook for 1 minute.

3 Fill the pigeons with the stuffing. Tuck the wings under the body, tie the legs together and close the cavity with a string and thick needle or secure with a toothpick.

4 In a separate pan boil 6^1/$_4$ cups water. Add the remaining onion, a pinch of salt, the cardamom pods, and squabs to the pan and simmer for 30 to 40 minutes over low heat until tender.

5 Preheat the oven to 400° F. Remove the squabs from the water, and unstring or remove the toothpicks. Transfer them to an oven-proof dish and bake for 30 to 40 minutes until browned. Transfer to a serving dish and garnish with the parsley. Serve hot.

SAUDI ARABIA

Kousy al-macarona
Spaghetti with chicken

SERVES 8

2 medium whole chickens
Salt, to taste
Vegetable oil for frying
6 tomatoes, peeled
$^1/_2$ cup yogurt
1 tsp black pepper
1 tsp ground cumin
3 cinnamon sticks
2 medium onions, peeled and chopped
1 tbsp olive oil
7 oz ground beef
6 medium potatoes, peeled and sliced into
  matchstick-sized pieces
1 lb 2 oz spaghetti
3 hard-boiled eggs, sliced
4 tbsp parsley, finely chopped

1 Cut each chicken into four pieces. Rinse thoroughly, pat dry and season with salt.

2 Heat 4 fl oz ($^1/_2$ cup) vegetable oil in a saucepan. Add the chicken pieces and fry for 5 minutes on each side. Drain some of the oil but keep the chicken in the pan.

3 In a bowl, purée the tomatoes and mix with the yogurt and half the quantity of spices. Pour this mixture over the chicken and simmer for about 40 minutes, until tender.

4 Cook the onions in the olive oil until tender, then add the ground beef and cook until brown. Season with salt, pepper, and the remaining cumin. Set aside.

5 Fry the potatoes in vegetable oil until browned on all sides. Remove from the oil and drain on paper towels.

6 Break the spaghetti into medium-sized pieces and cook in hot, salted water until just tender, then drain. Transfer the spaghetti to a serving dish. Arrange the chicken pieces on top and pour the sauce, potatoes, and sliced eggs over the meat. Sprinkle with parsley and serve immediately.

LEBANON

Shawarma dajaj
Baked chicken fingers

SERVES 5

2 lb 3 oz boned chicken breast, skinned
2 fl oz (¹/4 cup) lemon juice
4 fl oz (¹/2 cup) vegetable oil
¹/4 tsp of each: ground cloves, ground
   nutmeg, white pepper, allspice
¹/2 tsp sumac
¹/2 tsp oregano
¹/8 tsp ground mastic (optional)
3 garlic cloves, peeled and crushed
2 medium onions, peeled and chopped
Pita bread, garlic dip, grilled tomatoes,
   French fries, and lettuce leaves, to serve

1 Cut the chicken into Julienne strips. In a bowl, mix the chicken slices with all the other ingredients. Cover and marinate in the refrigerator overnight.

2 Preheat the oven to 400° F. Place the chicken with the marinade in an oven-proof dish. Cook in the oven for 20 to 30 minutes until tender. Serve with pita bread, garlic dip, grilled tomatoes, French fries, and lettuce leaves.

Garlic dip: In a bowl, pound 6 peeled garlic cloves with ¹/2 tsp salt to a smooth paste. In a separate bowl, mix 2 fl oz (¹/4 cup) lemon juice and 4 fl oz (¹/2 cup) vegetable oil together. Add this gradually to the garlic, blending thoroughly to obtain a homogenous fluid with the consistency of mayonnaise. Mix in 1 tbsp mayonnaise, if required.

SYRIA

SERVES 4–6

6 chicken breasts weighing about 3 lb 5 oz
$1/2$ cup all-purpose flour
$1/4$ cup ($1/2$ stick) butter
15 small onions, peeled
5 tbsp pine nuts
34 fl oz ($4^1/4$ cups) chicken stock
Pinch of salt
$1/4$ tsp black pepper
$1/4$ tsp cinnamon
3 tbsp lemon juice
Parsley sprigs, to garnish
Boiled white rice, to serve

Dajaj ablama
Chicken stew

1 Trim the chicken breasts of any fat, rinse, and pat dry. Cut each breast into 3 pieces and dip them in the flour. Melt the butter in a frying pan and fry the chicken pieces over moderate heat until brown on both sides. Remove the chicken from the pan.

2 Fry the whole onions in the same frying pan until golden brown. Remove, then fry the pine nuts until golden brown. Remove and drain on paper towels. Add the chicken stock, salt, pepper, and cinnamon to the pan, stirring continuously for 2 minutes.

3 Transfer the chicken and onions to a large saucepan. Add the stock and cook over moderate heat for about 40 minutes until tender. Add the lemon juice and cook for a further 5 minutes. Transfer to a serving dish and garnish with the fried pine nuts and parsley sprigs. Serve with boiled white rice.

 SAUDI ARABIA

SERVES 4

2 chicken breasts weighing about 1 lb 2 oz, skinned and deboned
Salt and black pepper, to taste
$5^1/4$ cups milk
1 tsp ground cardamom
$3/4$ cup superfine sugar
2 tbsp rose water
2 tbsp cornstarch
$1/2$ tsp cinnamon

Chicken stew

Sidreyat al dajaj
Flavored chicken breast

1 Place the chicken breasts in a saucepan and cover with cold water. Bring to a boil, skimming as required. Add the salt and pepper to taste, then cover and simmer gently for 40 minutes until well cooked.

2 Chop the chicken breasts into small pieces, then place in a blender or food processor with 1 cup of the milk and the cardamom. Blend, then and strain through a fine mesh sieve.

3 Place the remaining milk in a pan. Add the sugar and rose water and bring to a boil over low heat. Stir in the blended chicken. Add the cornstarch, stirring constantly until the mixture starts to thicken, then remove from the heat. Pour the mixture into a serving dish and leave aside to set. Sprinkle with the ground cinnamon and place in the refrigerator to cool.

EGYPT

SERVES 4–6

For the chicken

3 lb 5 oz chicken drumsticks, skinned
$^1/_2$ tsp black pepper
1 tsp cumin
$^1/_2$ tsp ground saffron
$^1/_2$ tsp hot red chili pepper
2 fl oz ($^1/_4$ cup) vegetable oil
1 medium onion, peeled and finely chopped
2 tsp cornstarch dissolved in 16 fl oz
  (2 cups) water
1 cinnamon stick
6 fresh dates, pitted
1 tbsp lemon juice

For the couscous

16 fl oz (2 cups) chicken stock
$^1/_2$ tsp ground saffron
10$^1/_2$ oz (2 cups) couscous
2$^1/_2$ oz ($^1/_2$ cup) whole blanched almonds,
  toasted, to garnish

Tajin al dajaj wil couscous

Chicken with couscous

1 Combine the chicken with the pepper, cumin, saffron, and chili pepper. Cover and marinate for 2 hours in the refrigerator.

2 Heat the vegetable oil in a frying pan and cook the chicken drumsticks until golden brown. Remove from the pan and set aside.

3 Heat the oil again in the same pan, add the onion, and cook until transparent. Return the chicken to the pan, and stir in the cornstarch and cinnamon stick. Cover and simmer gently for 40 minutes until tender.

4 In the meantime, make the saffron couscous: Boil the chicken stock and saffron in a saucepan. Remove from heat and stir in the couscous. Mix well and let stand for 5 minutes to absorb the liquid.

5 When the chicken is cooked, add the dates and the lemon juice to the pan and cook for a further 5 minutes. Transfer the couscous to a serving dish, place the chicken drumsticks on top of it, and sprinkle with toasted almonds.

UNITED ARAB EMIRATES

Dajaj biryani

Chicken biryani

SERVES 4–6

Medium whole chicken, cut into 8 pieces
8^1/$_2$ cups water
2 dried limes or the rind of 1 orange
2 chicken stock cubes
1 lb 2 oz (2^1/$_2$ cups) basmati rice, rinsed and
  drained
2 tbsp butter
3 medium onions, peeled and sliced
9 oz (1^1/$_8$ cup) yogurt
1 tsp cornstarch
^{3}/$_4$ tsp of each: black pepper, cumin, fresh
  cilantro, turmeric, cardamom, and
  cinnamon
3 garlic cloves, peeled and crushed
1 tsp ground saffron soaked in 2 fl oz
  (^{1}/$_4$ cup) hot water
Fried whole almonds, pine nuts, and
  pistachios, to garnish

1 Place the chicken pieces and water in a large saucepan. Bring to a boil, skimming whenever necessary. Add the dried limes or orange rind and the chicken stock cubes. Cover and simmer over low heat for 30 to 40 minutes until tender. Remove the chicken from the stock and set aside.

2 Add the rice to the stock in the pan and cook for 10 minutes until the rice is almost cooked. Drain and set aside.

3 Heat the butter in a large saucepan and fry the onions for 5 to 7 minutes, until golden brown. Stir in the cooked chicken.

4 In a bowl, mix the yogurt with the cornstarch. Strain through a sieve into a heavy saucepan. Place the pan over medium heat, stirring constantly in one direction with a wooden spoon until the yogurt starts to boil. Reduce the heat and simmer gently, uncovered, for 3 minutes, stirring occasionally. Add all the spices and garlic to the pan. Pour the boiled yogurt over the chicken. Add half the cooked rice to cover the chicken, then sprinkle with half the saffron water. Add the remaining rice and saffron water. Cover and simmer for 25 to 30 minutes until the rice is tender. Transfer to a large dish and garnish with fried almonds, pine nuts, and pistachios.

SAUDI ARABIA

SERVES 4–6

For the chicken
Medium whole chicken
6 1/3 cups water
2 chicken stock cubes
14 oz (2 cups) basmati or long-grain rice

For the sauce
2 tbsp vegetable oil
3 medium onions, peeled and finely sliced
1/2 cup yogurt
4 cardamom pods, bruised
1 tbsp fresh ginger, sliced
1 small cinnamon stick
1/2 tsp of each: black pepper and cumin
  powder
Pinch of ground saffron soaked in 2 fl oz
  (1/4 cup) of boiling water

Al roz al zerbian
Zerbian chicken

1 Cut the chicken into 8 pieces. Rinse thoroughly and pat dry. Place the chicken, water, and stock cubes in a large saucepan. Bring to the boil, skimming as necessary. Cover and leave to simmer over low heat for 45 minutes until tender.

2 Remove the chicken from the stock and set aside. Add the rice to the pan and bring to a boil. Simmer over medium heat for 10 minutes until the rice is half cooked, then drain.

3 To make the sauce, heat the vegetable oil in a medium-sized saucepan. Add the onions and fry for 6 to 8 minutes until golden brown. In a large bowl, mix the yogurt with all the spices. Carefully add the chicken to the yogurt mixture, and pour this over the onions in the saucepan. Pour the semi-cooked rice over the chicken mixture. Sprinkle with saffron water. Cover and simmer over low heat for 25 minutes until the rice is cooked. Transfer the rice and chicken to a serving dish and serve immediately.

IRAN

SERVES 4

3 tbsp vegetable oil
2 large onions, peeled and finely chopped
2 tsp turmeric powder
$^1/_2$ tsp black pepper
1 tsp lime powder or orange rind
Pinch of saffron
2 lb 3 oz chicken pieces with bones
3 tbsp tomato paste
5 cups water
7 oz (1 cup) canned chickpeas
Boiled rice, to serve

Gheymeh

Chicken with chickpeas

1 Heat the vegetable oil in a large saucepan and fry the onions for 4 to 5 minutes until tender. Add the turmeric powder, pepper, lime powder, saffron, and chicken pieces to the pan, stirring for 3 to 4 minutes. Add the tomato paste and stir for 1 to 2 minutes.

2 Add the water and bring to a boil, then reduce the heat. Cover and simmer for 20 minutes until the chicken is halfway cooked. Add the chickpeas and simmer for 45 minutes until the chicken and chickpeas are tender. Add more water if necessary. Serve with boiled rice.

 IRAQ

SERVES 4–6

Medium whole chicken
1 lemon, halved
Salt and black pepper, to taste
2 tbsp vegetable oil
10 garlic cloves, left whole and unpeeled
Juice of 1 lemon
34 fl oz (4$^1/_4$ cups) water
4 medium potatoes, peeled and cubed
1 tbsp cornstarch
Boiled white rice, to serve

Tashreeb dajaj

Pot roasted chicken

1 Rinse the chicken, drain, and pat dry. Rub it with the lemon halves, then season with salt and pepper and refrigerate for 30 minutes.

2 Heat the vegetable oil in a saucepan and cook the whole chicken until browned on all sides. Remove the outer layers of the garlic cloves but leave them unpeeled. Rinse and add to the chicken along with the lemon juice and water. Cover and simmer gently over low heat for 45 minutes. Add the potatoes and simmer for a further 15 minutes.

3 When tender, transfer the chicken to a platter and keep hot. Remove the garlic, keeping four cloves and discarding the rest. Add the cornstarch to the juices and reduce over high heat to 16 fl oz (2 cups). Peel the four garlic cloves, crush them and mix with the juices, adjusting the seasoning to taste. Cut the chicken into serving portions and pour the juices over the chicken. Serve hot with boiled white rice.

LEBANON

SERVES 5

Medium whole chicken, skinned and
  cut into 8 pieces
1 tsp salt
1/4 cup (1/2 stick) butter or 2 fl oz (1/4 cup)
  corn oil
6 1/3 cups hot water
1 cinnamon stick
1 small onion, peeled
1 parsley sprig
1 bay leaf
1/2 tsp of each: allspice, cinnamon powder,
  and black pepper
9 oz ground beef or lamb
2 tbsp butter
14 oz (2 cups) long-grain rice
5 tbsp blanched almonds
5 tbsp pine nuts

Djaj bel rouz

Chicken and rice

1 Rinse the chicken, drain, and rub it with the salt.

2 Heat the butter or oil in a frying pan. Add the chicken pieces and brown on both sides. Transfer the chicken pieces to a deep pan, cover with hot water and bring to a boil, skimming as necessary. Add the cinnamon stick, whole onion, parsley sprig, bay leaf, half the spices, and a pinch of salt. Cover and simmer over low heat for 45 minutes.

3 In another pan, fry the ground meat in 1 tablespoon butter until browned. Season with salt and the remainder of the spices. Add the rice, stirring for 2 minutes.

4 Measure 4 1/4 cups of the chicken stock from Step 2 and strain it into the rice and meat pan. Bring to a boil, then cover and simmer gently for 30 to 40 minutes until the rice is tender, stirring once or twice during cooking.

5 Brown the almonds and pine nuts in 1 tablespoon butter and set aside. Pour the rice onto a large platter, top with the chicken pieces, and sprinkle with almonds and pine nuts.

SAUDI ARABIA

SERVES 4–6

Medium whole chicken
4 fl oz ($1/2$ cup) corn oil
2 onions, peeled and finely chopped
$1/2$ tbsp of each: ground coriander, black
   pepper, and salt
1 red chili pepper
2 cups yogurt
1 cup water
1 tsp cornstarch
1 egg white
Boiled white rice, to serve

Dajaj bel laban
Chicken with yogurt

1 Rinse the chicken, remove the skin, and cut into 8 pieces. Heat the oil in a saucepan and fry the onions until tender. Add the chicken pieces and brown on both sides. Add the ground coriander, pepper, salt, and chili pepper. Cook over low heat for 45 minutes, stirring occasionally and adding small amounts of water as required.

2 Place the yogurt in a bowl and mix it with the water, cornstarch, and egg white. Strain through a sieve into a heavy pan. Place the pan over medium heat, stirring constantly in one direction with a wooden spoon until it starts to boil. Reduce the heat and simmer gently, uncovered, for 3 minutes, stirring occasionally.

3 When the chicken is cooked, add the yogurt mixture and continue to simmer over low heat for 15 minutes. Serve in a deep dish with boiled white rice.

SAUDI ARABIA

SERVES 4–5

Medium whole chicken, rinsed and
   cut into 8 pieces
1 cinnamon stick
2 cloves
3 black peppercorns
2 cardamom pods, bruised
1 bay leaf
1 fresh cilantro sprig
1 onion, peeled and quartered
2 cups milk
14 oz (2 cups) long-grain rice, rinsed
3 tbsp melted butter

Saliq dajaj
Chicken with milk and rice

1 Place the chicken pieces in a pot, cover with water, and bring to a boil, skimming as necessary. Add the cinnamon stick, cloves, peppercorns, cardamom pods, bay leaf, cilantro sprig, and onion. Cover and simmer over low heat for 45 minutes, until the chicken is tender.

2 Lift out the chicken and set aside. Add the milk and rice to the chicken stock and cook for 10 minutes until the rice is just tender.

3 Remove the bones from the chicken and cut into small pieces. Add the pieces to the rice and cook gently for 10 minutes, stirring once or twice. Place in a serving dish and drizzle with the melted butter.

Chicken with yogurt

KUWAIT

SERVES 6

Medium whole chicken
Salt and black pepper, to season
14 oz (2 cups) long-grain rice
2 fl oz (^{1}/$_4$ cup) vegetable oil
2 medium onions, peeled and sliced
12 oz (1^1/$_2$ cups) tomato purée
2 medium tomatoes, chopped
4 garlic cloves, peeled and crushed
6^1/$_3$ cups hot water
2 medium carrots, peeled and grated
Grated rind of 1 orange
4 cloves
4 cardamom pods
3 cinnamon sticks
4 tbsp raisins
4 tbsp slivered almonds

Kabsat al dajaj

Chicken with rice and tomatoes

1 Cut the chicken into 8 pieces. Rinse thoroughly, then pat dry and season with salt and pepper. Thoroughly rinse the rice and soak in salted water for about 30 minutes.

2 Heat the vegetable oil in a large saucepan. Add the onions and fry until golden brown. Add the chicken pieces, tomato purée, chopped tomatoes, and garlic, stirring for about 5 minutes over low heat.

3 Stir in the hot water, grated carrots, orange rind, spices, and salt and pepper, to taste. Cover and cook over medium heat for 40 minutes until the chicken is tender. Remove the chicken and keep in a warm place.

4 Add the rice to the liquid in the saucepan, cover and simmer for about 35 minutes until all the liquid has absorbed and rice is tender. Transfer the rice to the center of a serving platter and arrange the chicken pieces around it. Top with the raisins and almonds.

SYRIA

SERVES 4–6

10^1/$_2$ oz (1^1/$_2$ cups) dry chickpeas
1 tsp baking soda
Medium whole chicken, skinned and
  cut into 4 pieces
3 cups water
^{1}/$_2$ tsp of each: black pepper, cinnamon,
  and allspice
8 small onions, peeled and left whole
1 tsp salt
10^1/$_2$ oz (2 cups) coarse bulghur (coarse
  cracked wheat)
3 tbsp butter or corn oil
Yogurt or salad, to serve

Burghul bi dfeen

Cracked wheat with chicken

1 Place the chickpeas in a bowl and cover with water. Add the baking soda to the water and soak the chickpeas overnight. Drain the chickpeas and rinse under running water.

2 Place the chickpeas in a pan or a pressure cooker, cover with water, and bring to a boil. Cook over low heat for 30 to 45 minutes until half cooked.

3 Place the chicken pieces in another pan, cover with water, and bring to a boil, skimming as necessary. Cook for 5 minutes. Transfer the chicken to the chickpea pan, add all the spices, onions, and salt. Cover and cook for 20 to 30 minutes over low heat until both the chicken and chickpeas are tender.

4 Thoroughly rinse the bulghur and add it to the pan. If using a pressure cooker, do not close the lid firmly at this stage. Cook gently for 15 minutes until most of the liquid has been absorbed. Stir in the butter and cook for a further 5 minutes. Adjust seasoning. Serve hot with yogurt or salad.

KUWAIT

SERVES 4–5

Medium whole chicken
2 tbsp ghee or shortening
2 large onions, peeled and chopped
1 tbsp baharat spices (see page 158)
1 tsp turmeric
3 medium tomatoes, peeled and chopped
1/4 tsp cloves
1/2 tsp dried lime
2 cinnamon sticks
6 cardamom pods, bruised
3 tsp salt
32 fl oz (4 cups) water
14 oz (2 cups) basmati or long-grain rice
2 tbsp parsley, chopped
2 tbsp fresh cilantro, chopped

Machbous ala dajaj

Spiced chicken with rice

1 Cut the chicken into 8 pieces. Rinse thoroughly and pat dry.

2 Heat the ghee or shortening in a deep, heavy saucepan. Gently fry the onions until transparent and slightly brown. Stir in the baharat spices and turmeric and cook for 2 more minutes.

3 Stir in the chicken pieces and cook over medium heat until light brown. Add tomatoes, cloves, dried lime, cinnamon sticks, cardamom pods, and salt, stirring well. Then add the water, cover, and simmer gently for 30 to 40 minutes.

4 Place the rice in a bowl and rinse with cold water until the water runs clear, then drain. Gently stir the rice into the saucepan, add the herbs, and bring back to a slow simmer. If necessary add hot water to cover the rice and chicken. Cover and simmer over low heat for 30 minutes until the rice is tender, stirring gently once or twice during cooking. Remove from the heat and set aside to rest for 10 minutes. Transfer the rice to a large serving platter and place the chicken over the rice. Serve hot.

IRAN

SERVES 6

Medium whole chicken, cut into 8 pieces
4 fl oz (1/2 cup) vegetable oil
3 medium onions, peeled and thinly sliced
6 1/3 cups hot water
1 lb 2 oz fresh herbs (parsley, mint, fresh
  cilantro, and scallion)
2 garlic cloves, peeled and crushed
Salt, to taste
1 lb 2 oz ground walnuts
2 tbsp superfine sugar
16 fl oz (2 cups) fresh pomegranate juice, or
  2 fl oz (1/4 cup) pomegranate molasses
1 tsp cornstarch
1 tbsp walnuts, halved, to garnish
Boiled white rice, to serve

Khoesht anaar-aveej

Chicken with walnuts and herbs

1 Rinse the chicken pieces, drain, and pat dry. Heat the vegetable oil in a large saucepan. Add the onions and cook until tender. Add chicken pieces and cook until the color changes. Add the hot water and bring to a boil. Reduce the heat and simmer slowly for about 10 minutes.

2 Rinse and finely chop the herbs. In a separate pan, fry the herbs with the garlic in 1 tablespoon vegetable oil until tender, about 3 minutes. Transfer the herbs and garlic to the chicken pan and add the salt, ground walnuts, sugar, and pomegranate juice or molasses. Simmer for about 1 hour until the oil in the walnuts is released and sauce starts to thicken.

3 Dissolve the cornstarch in 2 fl oz (1/4 cup) cold water and add to the chicken, stirring for 2 minutes. Remove from heat and pour the chicken with the sauce into a serving platter and garnish with the walnuts. Serve hot with boiled white rice.

JORDAN

SERVES 2

Medium whole chicken
Salt, to taste
1/2 tsp allspice
1/2 tsp black pepper
4 fl oz (1/2 cup) olive oil
6 medium onions, peeled and sliced
3 tbsp sumac
2 pita bread (or thin flat bread)

Musakhan

Chicken roasted with bread

1 Clean the chicken and cut into two halves. Season with the salt, allspice, and pepper.

2 Heat half the olive oil in a large frying pan. Fry the two chicken pieces over medium heat until lightly browned on both sides. Transfer to a plate and set aside.

3 Add remaining olive oil to the pan with the onions. Fry gently, stirring often, until the onions are tender. Add the sumac and cook for 2 minutes, then remove from the heat.

4 Preheat the oven to 375° F. Split the pita bread into two parts and place in the bottom of a baking dish. Spread half the fried onions in the center of each pita bread half. Top each mound with a chicken half and spread the remaining onion mixture over each chicken half. Pour the oil from the pan over chicken. Cover the chicken completely with the remaining bread and sprinkle the bread with water.

5 Bake for 40 minutes, or until the chicken is tender and cooked through. When the bread begins to brown, sprinkle again lightly with water or cover the baking dish with a piece of tin foil. Serve hot.

FISH

For centuries, the inhabitants of the coastal areas surrounding the Mediterranean and the Gulf relied heavily on the bounty of the sea, and so fish played an important part in their diet. Today, fresh fish and seafood are a favorite choice because they are healthy: high in protein, low in fat, and a great source of essential vitamins.

The fish recipes in this section are succulent whether grilled, baked, fried, stuffed, minced, or prepared as a stew. You will find Sayyadiah (page 112), the delicately spiced fish served on a bed of rice, and Samke harrah (page 118), spicy fish lightly fried and baked in tahini sauce, in addition to many other mouthwatering recipes. No matter what your choice is, the fish should always be fresh.

LEBANON

SERVES 4–5

For the fish

2 lb 3 oz white fish filet, such as snapper,
  grouper, cod, or hake
4 tbsp olive oil
4 medium onions, peeled and chopped
5 garlic cloves, peeled and crushed
3 oz (1 cup) fresh cilantro, chopped
2 medium tomatoes, chopped
1 hot chili, chopped
1 tbsp tomato paste
4 oz (1 cup) walnuts, chopped
2 tbsp pine nuts

For the sauce

2 fl oz (1/4 cup) tahini
2 fl oz (1/4 cup) lemon juice
2 fl oz (1/4 cup) water
Salt and black pepper, to taste
Bread, to serve

Samak bi taratour

Fish with tahini sauce and walnuts

1 Preheat the oven to 400° F. Start by preparing the fish. Rinse the filets and pat dry with paper towels. Place them in a greased oven-proof dish and cook in the oven for about 25 minutes, until tender.

2 Heat 2 tablespoons olive oil in a frying pan and fry the onions until golden brown. Add the garlic, cilantro, tomatoes, chili, and tomato paste. Bring to a boil for 2 minutes, then remove from heat.

3 To make the tahini sauce, combine all the sauce ingredients together. Add the sauce to the pan with the onion mixture and return to heat, stirring continuously until it starts to boil. Remove from heat.

4 In a separate frying pan, brown the walnuts in 2 tablespoons olive oil, then remove from the heat. Add the pine nuts to the oil and brown.

5 To serve, place the fish filet on a platter, top with the tahini sauce, and garnish with the walnuts and pine nuts. Serve with bread.

LEBANON

SERVES 6

3 lb 5 oz red snapper or any other large fish,
  such as sea bream, hake, or cod
1/2 tsp salt
9 fl oz (1 1/8 cups) olive oil
7 medium onions, peeled and sliced
  lengthwise
1 tsp black pepper
1 tbsp cumin
34 fl oz (4 1/4 cups) hot water
Juice of 2 lemons
2 tbsp pomegranate molasses
1 lb 5 oz (3 cups) long-grain rice,
  rinsed and drained
2 1/2 oz (1/2 cup) pine nuts
2 1/2 oz (1/2 cup) whole almonds, blanched
2 tbsp vegetable oil

Sayyadiah

Fish with rice

1 Scale, clean, and rinse the fish. Pat it dry with paper towels and sprinkle the surface and cavities with the salt. Cover and refrigerate for 30 minutes.

2 Heat the olive oil in a deep pan. Brown the fish over high heat, about 7 minutes on each side. Remove from the heat, then remove the fish bones, skin, and heads (save the latter). Cut the fish into serving pieces and set aside.

3 Fry the onions in the same oil over low heat for about 15 minutes, until golden brown. Remove half the onions and set aside for garnishing. Continue cooking the remaining onions for another 5 minutes until dark brown. Add the fish heads, pepper, cumin, and hot water. Cover and simmer gently for 30 minutes. Then discard the fish heads. Stir the onion mixture well, then add the lemon juice and pomegranate molasses. Heat until boiling.

4 Add the rice to the pan with the onion mixture, cover and cook over low heat for 25 to 30 minutes until tender. Add more hot water if needed.

5 Brown the pine nuts and almonds in the vegetable oil. Lift and drain on paper towels. Pour the rice on a serving dish. Top with the fish pieces and sprinkle with the reserved onions, pine nuts, and almonds. Serve hot.

KUWAIT

SERVES 4–5

For the shrimp paste
2 lb 3 oz raw shrimp, shelled and deveined
7 oz (1 cup) ground rice
3 tbsp fresh cilantro, chopped
1/2 tsp turmeric
1/2 tsp salt

For the stuffing
1 tbsp butter
2 medium onions, peeled and chopped
7 oz raw shrimp, shelled and chopped
1 tsp baharat spices (see page 158)
1 tsp dried lime or grated rind of 1 lemon
1/2 tsp salt
2 tbsp raisins

For the sauce
1 tbsp butter
2 medium onions, peeled and chopped
2 garlic cloves, peeled and crushed
2 tbsp fresh cilantro, chopped
2 medium tomatoes, peeled and chopped
1 tsp baharat spices (see page 158)
1/2 tsp salt
2 tbsp tamarind, soaked in 2 cups
  warm water

Boiled white rice, to serve

Kebab al rubyan

Shrimp balls

1 Start by preparing the shrimp paste. Rinse and dry the shrimp. Using a food processor, process the shrimp with ground rice, cilantro, turmeric, and salt until thoroughly blended. Cover and refrigerate for 30 minutes.

2 To make the stuffing, melt the butter in a pan and gently fry onions until tender. Add the chopped shrimp, baharat spices, dried lime or lemon rind, salt, and raisins. Cook until the shrimp pieces are tender. Remove from heat and set aside.

3 To make the tamarind sauce, melt the butter in a pan and gently fry onions and garlic until tender. Add the cilantro, tomatoes, baharat spices, and salt and cook for 2 minutes. Strain the tamarind liquid and add it to the sauce. Cover and simmer gently for 20 minutes.

4 In the meantime, prepare the shrimp balls. Take a piece of shrimp paste the size of an egg and flatten with moistened hands to a 4-inch patty. Place a tablespoon of stuffing in the center of the patty, then close it up, shaping it into a ball. Repeat with the remaining ingredients.

5 Gently drop the shrimp balls into the simmering tamarind sauce. Cover and simmer for 30 minutes. When cooked, remove the balls from the sauce with a slotted spoon and serve hot on a bed of white rice. Pour some of the sauce over the rice.

UNITED ARAB EMIRATES

SERVES 5

1/2 cup all-purpose flour
1/4 tsp salt
Pinch of black pepper
2 lb 3 oz hamour fish or white fish filets
4 fl oz (1/2 cup) olive oil
2 medium onions, peeled and thinly sliced
1 green pepper, cut into long thin strips
2 tbsp parsley
Lemon wedges, to garnish
Baked potatoes, to serve

Samak bil khidar
Fried fish with vegetables

1 Combine the flour, salt, and pepper. Dip the fish filets in the flour mixture to coat lightly.

2 Heat half the olive oil in a large frying pan. Add the fish and fry until tender and browned on both sides, for about 10 minutes, then remove and place on a platter. Keep warm.

3 Pour the remaining olive oil into the frying pan. Add the onions, green pepper, and parsley. Cook until the onions are tender, and season with salt and pepper to taste. Spoon the onion mixture over the fish and garnish with lemon wedges. Serve hot with baked potatoes.

 SAUDI ARABIA

SERVES 5–6

2 lb 3 oz raw shrimp, shelled and deveined
Pinch of salt
1 tbsp all-purpose four
14 oz (2 cups) rice
34 fl oz (4 1/4 cups) hot water
8 fl oz (1 cup) tomato juice
1/2 tsp each of cinnamon, cardamom, and
   black pepper
Salt, to taste
2 fl oz (1/4 cup) corn oil
2 medium onions, peeled and chopped

Roz bel jamberry
Rice with shrimp

1 Thoroughly rinse the shrimp and rub with the salt and flour. Set aside.

2 Thoroughly rinse the rice. Cook in a saucepan with the hot water, tomato juice, all the spices and salt, to taste, over low heat for about 25 minutes until tender.

3 Heat the corn oil in a frying pan and fry the onions until golden brown. Add the shrimp and cook for 3 minutes on each side. Add the cooked rice to the shrimp and simmer over low heat for 5 minutes. Serve hot.

Fried fish with vegetables

LEBANON

SERVES 5

1 large snapper or grouper fish weighing
   about 4 lb 6 oz
1/2 tsp salt
4 fl oz (1/2 cup) vegetable oil
10 garlic cloves, peeled
11/2 oz (1/2 cup) fresh cilantro,
   finely chopped
1 tbsp ground coriander
1 hot red chili, chopped
8 fl oz (1 cup) tahini
16 fl oz (2 cups) cold water
6 fl oz (3/4 cup) lemon juice
4 tbsp pine nuts

Samke harrah

Spicy fish

1 Clean and scale the fish. Rub it with the salt, then cover and refrigerate for 2 hours.

2 Heat the vegetable oil in a large frying pan. Add the fish and fry over high heat for 3 to 4 minutes on each side. Carefully transfer the fish to an oven-proof dish along with 2 tablespoons of the frying oil.

3 Preheat the oven to 400° F. In a small bowl, crush the garlic cloves with 1/2 teaspoon salt. Mix with the fresh cilantro and ground coriander and half the chili. Stuff the fish cavity with half the garlic mixture.

4 Place the tahini in a small bowl, then gradually add the water, beating continuously. Stir in the lemon juice and the remaining garlic mixture. Pour the sauce over the fish. If the sauce doesn't cover the fish completely, add a little more water. Cook in the oven for 20 to 25 minutes until the fish is tender and the sauce is bubbling.

5 In the meantime, heat 1 tablespoon vegetable oil in a small frying pan and fry the pine nuts until golden brown. Carefully transfer the fish to a platter. Top with the cooking juices and sprinkle with the pine nuts. Serve hot.

EGYPT

SERVES 5

2 lb 3 oz fresh sardines
5 garlic cloves, peeled
1 tbsp salt
1/4 tsp black pepper
1/2 tsp cumin
8 fl oz (1 cup) lemon juice
1 hot red chili pepper
6 fl oz (3/4 cup) vegetable oil
3 medium tomatoes, sliced into thick rings
2 green peppers, sliced into thin rings
3 lemons, sliced into rings

Sardine bil forn

Baked sardines

1 Remove the guts and head of the sardines. Rinse thoroughly, then drain.

2 Crush the garlic with the salt. Stir in the pepper, cumin, lemon juice, and chili. Marinate the sardines in this mixture for 1 hour.

3 Preheat the oven to 375° F. Transfer the fish with marinade to a baking dish and pour the vegetable oil over it. Top with the tomatoes, the green peppers, and the lemon slices.

4 Cook in the oven for 30 to 40 minutes, until the fish is cooked and golden brown. Serve hot or cold with tahini sauce.

YEMEN

SERVES 5–6

2 lb 3 oz white fish filet, such as cod, hake, or hamour, cut into serving pieces
4 tbsp fresh cilantro, chopped
2 tbsp fresh dill, chopped
4 tbsp vegetable oil
1 tbsp salt
2 medium onions, peeled and thinly sliced
1 green chili, chopped
3 medium tomatoes, chopped
8 fl oz (1 cup) hot water
1/2 tsp of each: allspice, cumin, black pepper, and cardamom
Boiled white rice, to serve

Matfiya

Fried fish with onion and tomato

1 In a bowl, combine the fish filet with 2 tablespoons cilantro, the dill, 1 tablespoon vegetable oil, and salt. Cover and marinate for 1 hour in the refrigerator.

2 Heat the remaining oil in a large frying pan. Add the fish, stirring frequently for about 6 minutes, until golden brown.

3 Add the onions, chili, and tomatoes to the pan and cook for a further 8 minutes. Stir in the hot water with the remaining cilantro and all the spices. Bring to a boil, then reduce the heat and simmer for 10 minutes. Serve hot with boiled white rice.

Baked sardines

UNITED ARAB EMIRATES

SERVES 4

2 lb 3 oz shrimp, shelled and deveined
Salt, to taste
3 tbsp all-purpose flour
2 tbsp butter
2 tsp olive oil
1 large onion, peeled and chopped
3 garlic cloves, peeled and crushed
3 tbsp fresh cilantro, chopped
Juice of 1 lemon
Cilantro sprigs, to garnish
Boiled rice and sautéed vegetables, to serve

Rubyan

Garlic shrimp

1 Sprinkle the shrimp with salt, then dip them in flour to coat.

2 Melt the butter and olive oil in a large frying pan. Add the onion and garlic and cook until tender. Add the shrimp and cilantro. Cook, stirring regularly, until the shrimp are golden brown, for about 5 minutes.

3 Transfer the shrimp to a platter, sprinkle with the lemon juice, and garnish with sprigs of cilantro. Serve hot with boiled rice and sautéed vegetables.

 EGYPT

SERVES 4–5

2 lb 3 oz hamour or white fish filet, such as
  cod or flounder
Juice of 1 lemon
Pinch of salt
$1/4$ tsp black pepper
$1/4$ tsp allspice
4 fl oz ($1/2$ cup) corn oil
5 medium onions, peeled and sliced
16 fl oz (2 cups) tomato juice
5 garlic cloves, peeled and chopped
2 tbsp ground coriander
Salt, to taste
8 fl oz (1 cup) water
3 tbsp all-purpose flour

Kozbariet al samak

Fish filet with coriander

1 Rinse the fish and pat it dry with paper towels. In a bowl, mix the lemon juice, salt, pepper, and allspice. Place the filets in the bowl and toss gently until well coated. Cover and refrigerate for 2 hours.

2 Heat 2 tablespoons corn oil in a frying pan. Add the onions and cook until tender. Stir in the tomato juice, garlic, coriander, salt, and water. Bring to a boil, then reduce the heat. Simmer gently for 20 minutes until sauce has thickened.

3 Preheat the oven to 400° F. Dip the filets in the flour to coat them and fry in hot corn oil until lightly browned on both sides. Spread half the quantity of tomato sauce in a 12-inch oven-proof dish. Arrange the fish filets on top, then pour the remaining tomato sauce over the top. Cook in the oven for 30 minutes until golden brown. Serve hot.

EGYPT

Tagin samak
Baked fish

SERVES 5

2 lb 3 oz seabass filet, sliced into 5 pieces
1 tbsp salt
$^1/_4$ tsp black pepper
$^1/_4$ tsp cumin
Juice of 2 lemons
4 fl oz ($^1/_2$ cup) corn oil
$^1/_2$ cup all-purpose flour
3 medium onions, peeled and chopped
3 green peppers, coarsely chopped
4 garlic cloves, peeled and crushed
16 fl oz (2 cups) fresh tomato juice
1 tbsp tomato paste
$^1/_2$ tsp dried cilantro
3 oz (1 cup) fresh cilantro, chopped
$1^1/_2$ oz ($^1/_2$ cup) dill, chopped
2 medium tomatoes, thickly sliced
Boiled, buttered rice, to serve

1 Place the fish slices in a bowl. Add the salt, pepper, half the cumin, lemon juice, 4 tablespoons of the corn oil, and the flour. Toss gently to coat the fish pieces. Cover and marinate for 2 hours.

2 Preheat the oven to 375° F. Transfer the fish pieces with the marinade to an oven-proof dish. Cover and cook in the oven for 10 minutes.

3 Heat the remaining corn oil in a frying pan. Stir in the onions, green peppers, and garlic and cook for 5 minutes. Before the vegetables start browning, add the tomato juice, tomato paste, remaining cumin, and dried cilantro and cook for 5 more minutes over medium heat. Add the fresh cilantro and dill and cook for 1 minute.

4 Divide the mixture into two equal portions. Evenly spread one portion of the mixture in an oven-proof dish. Add a layer of partly cooked fish and cover with the second half of the mixture, then top with tomato slices. Cook in the oven for 15 minutes. Serve with boiled, buttered rice.

LEBANON

Sultan Ibrahim Mikli
Fried red mullet

SERVES 3–4

10–12 red mullets
1 tbsp salt
3 tbsp all-purpose flour
8 fl oz (1 cup) vegetable oil, for deep frying
Baked potatoes, salad, and bread, to serve

1 Clean and scale the fish. Rinse and thoroughly drain. Rub the fish inside and out with the salt. Cover and refrigerate for 1 hour so that the fish absorbs the salt.

2 Sprinkle the fish with the flour. Heat the vegetable oil in a frying pan and fry the fish over high heat for 5 to 7 minutes on each side, until tender and golden brown. Carefully lift the fish out of the pan and drain on paper towels. Serve warm with baked potatoes, salad, and bread.

KUWAIT

SERVES 4–5

2 tbsp vegetable oil
2 lb 3 oz raw shrimp, shelled and deveined
4 garlic cloves, peeled and crushed
1 medium onion, peeled and chopped
1 tsp baharat spices (see page 158)
Pinch of ground hot red chili
1 tsp turmeric
1 tbsp parsley, chopped
2 tbsp fresh cilantro, chopped
2 medium tomatoes, peeled and chopped
2 tsp salt
Black pepper, to taste
17 fl oz (2 1/8 cups) water
14 oz (2 cups) basmati or long-grain rice
Salad, to serve

Machbous ala rubyan

Spiced shrimp

1 In a large saucepan, heat the vegetable oil and add the shrimp and garlic. Fry over moderate heat until the shrimp turn pink, for about 2 minutes on each side. Remove from the heat and set side.

2 Stir in the onion and cook gently until tender and browned. Season with the baharat spices, chili, and turmeric.

3 Add the parsley, cilantro, tomatoes, salt, pepper, and water. Bring to a boil, then cover and cook over moderate heat for 3 to 4 minutes.

4 Rinse the rice until the water runs clear. Add it to the saucepan, bring to a boil, then cover and cook for 12 minutes. Add more water if necessary. Add the shrimp to the rice, stirring lightly. Cover and simmer gently over low heat for 20 minutes. Stir, remove from the heat, and leave covered for 5 minutes. Transfer to a serving dish. Serve hot with salad.

IRAQ

SERVES 6

1 whole perch, trout, or carp weighing
  about 3 lb 5 oz
4 tbsp vegetable oil
3 large onions, peeled and thinly sliced
5 garlic cloves, peeled and crushed
1 tsp curry powder
1 tsp ground dried lime or
  grated rind of 1 lemon
2 tsp salt
2 tbsp tamarind paste
8 fl oz (1 cup) warm water
3 tbsp parsley, chopped
3 tbsp fresh cilantro, chopped
Green salad, to serve

Samak mishwi
Oven barbecued fish

1 Clean and scale the fish. Cut it open lengthways from the head to the tail through the back. Rinse and pat dry with paper towels. Place the fish under the broiler for 5 minutes on each side until partially cooked, then transfer to an oven-proof dish.

2 In the meantime, heat the vegetable oil in a frying pan. Fry the onions and garlic, stirring occasionally until tender. Stir in the curry powder, dried lime or lemon rind, and salt.

3 Dissolve the tamarind paste in the warm water and add it to the onion mixture. Cook over medium heat for 25 minutes, until it becomes a thick paste. Add the parsley and cilantro.

4 Preheat the oven to 400° F. Spread the onion mixture over the grilled fish. Cook in the oven for 15 to 20 minutes until the fish is cooked. Then place the fish under the broiler for 1 minute until a thin crust has formed on the stuffing. Serve hot with a green salad.

EGYPT

Kofta al samak
Minced fish

SERVES 5

2 lb 3 oz white fish filet, such as hamour or cod
6 1/3 cups water
1 tsp salt
1 lb 2 oz potatoes, peeled and kept whole
2 garlic cloves, peeled and chopped
5 tbsp fresh cilantro, chopped
1 tsp black pepper
5 tbsp parsley, chopped
1/2 tsp cinnamon
1 medium onion, peeled and finely chopped
1 beaten egg
1/4 cup breadcrumbs
3 tbsp vegetable oil
Salad, bread, or boiled rice, to serve
Wedge of lemon, to garnish

1 Place the fish in a saucepan. Add the water and salt and bring to a boil. Reduce the heat and poach the fish gently for 15 minutes. When cooked, gently remove the fish with a slotted spoon and reserve the liquid. Cook the potatoes in the fish water for 15 minutes.

2 Mince the fish and the boiled potatoes using a fork or a food processor. Add the garlic, cilantro, pepper, parsley, cinnamon, and onions and mix thoroughly. Divide the resulting paste into 30 balls each the size of a small egg. Flatten them into patties and dip in the beaten egg, then coat with breadcrumbs.

3 Fry the fish patties in the hot vegetable oil until brown on both sides. Serve hot with a salad and bread or boiled white rice. Garnish with a wedge of lemon.

 BAHRAIN

Samak mishwi bil asiakh
Fish on skewers

SERVES 4–5

For the fish
2 lb 3 oz hamour or 12 red mullet
1 tbsp all-purpose flour
2 tbsp lemon juice
1 tbsp salt
8 fl oz (1 cup) vegetable oil, for deep frying

For the marinade
1 tbsp fresh coriander, chopped
4 fl oz (1/2 cup) white wine vinegar
1 tsp white pepper
1/2 tsp cinnamon
1 tsp cumin

Parsley sprigs, to garnish
1 lemon, cut into wedges, to garnish

1 Rinse the fish and pat it dry with paper towels. Rub it with the flour, lemon, and salt.

2 To make the marinade, mix all the marinade ingredients together in a bowl. Add the fish and toss gently to coat. Cover and marinate for about 2 hours in the refrigerator.

3 Thread the whole fish onto bamboo skewers. Heat the vegetable oil in a frying pan and deep-fry the fish for 6 to 7 minutes on both sides until golden brown. Remove and drain on paper towels.

4 Transfer the fish onto a serving dish. Serve with fried potato rings and toasted bread, and garnish with parsley sprigs and lemon wedges.

YEMEN

SERVES 4–5

2 lb 3 oz whole hamour, or seabass, halibut,
  or cod, cleaned and cut into cutlets
$1/2$ tsp of each: cumin, coriander, black
  pepper, cinnamon, and turmeric
Salt, to taste
1 lb 2 oz ($2^1/2$ cups) basmati or
  long-grain rice
34 fl oz ($4^1/4$ cups) hot water
3 tbsp vegetable oil
2 medium onions, peeled and thinly sliced
2 garlic cloves, peeled and crushed

Sanouna
Hamour fish cutlets

1 Season the fish cutlets with all the spices and salt. Cover and refrigerate for 30 minutes.

2 Place the rice and water in a pan and bring to a boil. Cook over medium heat for 10 minutes until the water has been absorbed and the rice is half cooked. Set aside.

3 Heat the vegetable oil in a frying pan. Fry the fish cutlets until golden brown on both sides. Remove from the heat and set aside. In the same pan, stir in the onions and cook over medium heat for 5 minutes until golden brown. Add the garlic, stirring for 2 minutes.

4 Place half the cooked rice over the onions and top with the fish cutlets, then cover with the remaining rice. Sprinkle the rice with a little water, cover and simmer gently for 20 minutes until tender. Transfer the rice onto a large serving dish, making sure not to break the fish, and place the fish cutlets on top. Serve hot.

KUWAIT

SERVES 4–5

10$^1/_2$ oz (1$^1/_2$ cups) lentils
34 fl oz (4$^1/_4$ cups) water
3 tbsp vegetable oil
2 medium onions, peeled and chopped
2–3 garlic cloves, peeled and crushed
2 lb 3 oz raw shrimp, shelled and deveined
1 tsp dried lime or lemon peel
Pinch of black pepper
Pinch of turmeric
Pinch of cardamom
5 cloves
3 oz (1 cup) fresh cilantro, chopped
14 oz (2 cups) long-grain rice, rinsed
Salt, to taste
Lemon slices, to garnish

Marbeen

Shrimp with lentils and rice

1 Rinse the lentils and place them in a saucepan with the water. Bring to a boil and cook over moderate heat for 20 minutes.

2 Heat the vegetable oil in a frying pan and add half the onions. Cook until golden brown, then add the garlic, stirring for 2 minutes.

3 Add half the shrimp, dried lime or lemon peel, pepper, turmeric, cardamom, and cloves to the onions, stirring for 5 minutes. Stir in half the cilantro, cover, and simmer over low heat for 5 minutes, until tender.

4 Add the shrimp mixture to the lentils, then add the rice. Adjust the water quantity as needed to cover the rice and lentil mixture. Simmer over low heat for about 30 minutes until the lentils and rice are tender and the sauce has thickened.

5 Fry the second half of the shrimp in vegetable oil for 3 minutes on each side. Add the remaining onion and cilantro and season with salt and pepper. Cook for 3 minutes until tender, then remove from the heat and set aside.

6 Pour the lentil and rice mixture into a serving dish. Garnish with the fried shrimp and lemon slices.

IRAN

SERVES 5–6

1 lb 2 oz sole steaks
Pinch of salt
3 tbsp vegetable oil
1/4 tsp turmeric
3 red peppers, deseeded and cubed
4 tbsp fresh cilantro, chopped
4 tbsp parsley, chopped
2 tbsp dill, chopped
1 large onion, peeled and chopped
6 cardamom pods
6 cloves
1 bay leaf
Black pepper, to taste
14 oz (2 cups) basmati rice, rinsed
34 fl oz (4 1/4 cups) boiling water
Juice of 1 lemon
Fresh cilantro, to garnish

Mohi polou

Sole steaks with herbed rice

1 Rinse the fish steaks, dry them with paper towels, and sprinkle lightly with salt. Set aside for 20 minutes to absorb the salt.

2 Heat the vegetable oil in a pan and fry the fish steaks for 4 minutes on each side over high heat. Transfer to a plate.

3 Add the turmeric, red peppers, cilantro, parsley, and dill to the pan and fry for 2 minutes, then lift from the pan.

4 Add the onion to the pan, stirring until golden brown. Add the cardamom pods, cloves, bay leaf, and pepper, stirring for 1 minute, then add the rice and stir for 3 minutes. Season with salt.

5 Pour the boiling water over the rice and bring to a boil. Reduce the heat and simmer for 10 minutes, until half cooked. Remove half the rice from the pan and arrange the fish steaks on top of the rice in the pan. Sprinkle with the pepper mixture. Top with the remainder of the rice and lemon juice. Cover and simmer gently for 10 minutes. Transfer to a serving dish and serve hot, garnished with cilantro.

DESSERTS

The following pages showcase a selection of delicious and simple-to-make sweet treats for any occasion. Ma'amoul (page 154), semolina cakes stuffed with a nut filling, are eaten to celebrate holidays. For festive occations, try Baklawa (page 138), the filo pastry stuffed with nuts, or Atayef bil ashta (page 141), the thick pancakes oozing with a deliciously rich cottage cheese mixture topped with a sweet sugar syrup. Many of the desserts featured in the following pages are very simple and can be prepared in advance.

LEBANON

SERVES 4–6

1 tbsp cornstarch
3 tbsp superfine sugar
17 fl oz (2^1/8 cups) milk
1 gelatin leaf (equal to ^{1}/4 packet gelatin)
1 tsp rose water
1 tbsp orange-flower water
2 oz (^{1}/3 cup) ground almonds, to garnish
2 oz (^{1}/3 cup) ground pistachios, to garnish

Muhallabia

Milk pudding

1 Dissolve the cornstarch, sugar, and 2 fl oz (^{1}/4 cup) of the milk in a heavy pan. Stir in the remaining milk and bring to a boil. Reduce the heat and simmer gently for 10 minutes, stirring constantly.

2 Add the gelatin leaf to the pan and simmer for a further 10 minutes. Then add the rose water and orange-flower water, stirring for 1 minute. Remove from the heat and set aside until the mixture cools a little, then pour into a bowl. Cover and refrigerate for 3 or more hours. Turn the pudding onto a serving dish and garnish with almonds and pistachios.

 KUWAIT

SERVES 8

7 oz (1^1/2 cups) raisins
10^1/2 oz dried apricots
2 tbsp clear runny honey
34 fl oz (4^1/4 cups) water
1 tsp lemon juice
1 tbsp rose water
1 tbsp orange-flower water
^{1}/2 cup superfine sugar
3^1/2 oz (^{1}/2 cup) blanched almonds
3^1/2 oz (^{1}/2 cup) pistachios
3^1/2 oz (^{1}/2 cup) pine nuts

Khoshaf

Dried fruit

1 Rinse the raisins and dried apricots and drain. Place them in a bowl with the honey and water. Cover and chill for 4 hours, then transfer to a serving bowl.

2 Dissolve the sugar in a little water. Stir in the lemon juice, rose water, and orange-flower water. Add to the dried fruit and toss to ensure that the fruit is coated in this mixture. Sprinkle with the nuts and serve cold with your choice of fruit juice.

Aish al saraya

Sweet bread

SERVES 8

1 lb 10 oz white bread, preferably unsalted
4 cups superfine sugar
17 fl oz (2^1/$_8$ cups) water
1 tsp lemon juice
1 tbsp orange-flower water
1 lb 2 oz Ashta or ricotta cheese
^{3}/$_4$ cup whipped cream
7 oz (1 cup) ground pistachios

1 Remove the bread crusts with a sharp knife and discard. Toast the bread in a hot oven until lightly golden brown. Cool and break into very small pieces.

2 Place 1 cup of the sugar in a saucepan and dissolve over moderate heat, stirring constantly with a wooden spoon until golden brown. Add the water and the remaining sugar, stirring until dissolved. Leave over moderate heat for 5 minutes without stirring.

3 Add the lemon juice and bread pieces to the pan. Stir for 3 minutes until the bread absorbs all the sugar syrup and becomes soft. Add the orange-flower water and remove from the heat.

4 Pour the mixture in a large serving dish and crush any pieces that are still hard to a paste-like consistency. Flatten the surface with the back of a spoon and leave to cool.

5 In a bowl, mix the Ashta or ricotta cheese with the whipped cream. Spread evenly over the bread-syrup mixture, then sprinkle with a thick layer of pistachios. Chill for 1 hour. Cut and serve.

IRAN

Ranginak

Date fudge

SERVES 4

11¹/2 oz (2⁷/8 sticks) butter
3³/4 cups all-purpose flour
³/4 cup superfine sugar
1 tsp ground cinnamon
¹/2 tsp cardamom
3¹/2 oz (1 cup) walnuts, halved
1 lb 2 oz pitted dates
1 tsp ground pistachios

1 Melt the butter over medium heat in a heavy saucepan. Add the flour, stirring constantly, until golden brown. Remove from heat and cool slightly. Add the sugar, cinnamon, and cardamom to the flour and butter and mix together well.

2 Pour half the flour mixture into a flat 10-inch round dish and flatten the surface with the back of a spoon. Insert half a walnut inside each date and place the dates on top of the flour mixture. Cover the dates with the remaining flour mixture and again flatten the surface with the back of a spoon. Cut into diamond shapes. Sprinkle with ground pistachios and serve cold.

LEBANON

MAKES ABOUT 40 PIECES

For the pastry
1 lb 2 oz (22 sheets) filo pastry
7 tbsp unsalted butter, melted

For the nut filling
9 oz (2 cups) coarsely ground almonds,
  walnuts, or pine nuts
1/2 cup superfine sugar
1 tsp orange-flower water

For the sugar syrup
2 cups superfine sugar
12 fl oz (1 1/2 cups) water
1 tsp lemon juice
2 tsp orange-flower water

Baklawa

Filo stuffed with nuts

1 Allow the filo pastry to reach room temperature before using. Brush a large baking dish with a little melted butter. Trim the edges of the filo pastry to fit the size of the dish. Place a sheet of filo in the baking dish. Brush it with butter and top with another sheet, keeping the remainder covered with a damp towel. Repeat in the same manner until half (approximately 10) of the filo sheets are used.

2 Preheat the oven to 375° F. To make the filling, combine the nuts with the sugar and orange-flower water. Spread the nut filling over the filo sheets in the baking dish. Place a sheet of filo over the filling, brush with butter, and repeat in the same manner until all sheets are used. Brush the top layer with butter and cut the layers into diamond shapes with a sharp knife. Bake for 1 hour until the top is lightly colored. Drain any excess fat.

3 In the meantime, make the sugar syrup. Add the sugar and water to a saucepan, stirring over medium heat until dissolved. Simmer for 15 minutes without stirring, then stir in the lemon juice and orange-flower water just before removing from heat. When the syrup has cooled, pour it over the hot pastry and set aside to cool. Cut the pastry and store at room temperature in an airtight container.

LEBANON

MAKES 16–18 PANCAKES

For the batter
1 tsp active dry yeast
1 tsp superfine sugar
4 fl oz (^{1}/$_2$ cup) warm water
2^1/$_4$ cups all-purpose flour
Pinch of salt
12 fl oz (1^1/$_2$ cups) milk
^{1}/$_4$ cup (^{1}/$_2$ stick) butter

For the filling
1 lb 2 oz Ashta or cottage cheese
2 oz (^{1}/$_3$ cup) ground pistachios
2 tbsp preserved orange blossoms

For the sugar syrup
2 cups superfine sugar
12 fl oz (1^1/$_2$ cups) water
1 tsp lemon juice
2 tsp orange-flower water

Atayef bil ashta

Pancakes with cream

1 Start by making the batter. In a mixing bowl, dissolve the yeast and sugar in the warm water. Sift the flour and salt into the bowl and gradually stir in the milk, beating until smooth. Cover the bowl and set aside to rest in a warm place for 1 hour until the batter has risen and doubled in size.

2 Heat a small, heavy frying pan over medium heat and grease very lightly with butter. Spoon the batter into a piping bag fitted with a round tip. Squeeze the batter into the pan and tilt immediately so that the batter spreads into a circle approximately 4 inches in diameter. The pancake should be about ^{1}/$_4$ inch thick.

3 Cook for about 1 minute until golden brown on the underside. Flip over and cook for a few seconds on the other side. Lift out and place on a plate, covering with a damp cloth to prevent drying. Repeat until all the batter has been used, stacking the pancakes one on top of the other.

4 Place 1 tablespoon of Ashta or cottage cheese on the pale side of the pancake. Fold over and press together half the edge, leaving the other half open with the Ashta protruding from it. Garnish with the ground pistachios and preserved orange blossoms.

5 To make the sugar syrup, add the sugar and water to a saucepan, stirring over medium heat until dissolved. Simmer for 15 minutes without stirring, then stir in the lemon juice and orange-flower water just before removing from heat. When the syrup has cooled, drizzle over the pancakes.

SAUDI ARABIA

SERVES 6–8

2 cups superfine sugar
8 fl oz (1 cup) water
1 tsp lemon juice
1 tsp cardamom powder
2 oz ($^1/_3$ cup) ground unsalted peanuts
$10^1/_2$ oz (3 cups) whole milk powder

Halawa labanieh
Cream and nut sweets

1 Place the sugar, water, and lemon juice in a large saucepan. Cook over low heat for 15 minutes until the syrup has thickened. Remove from the heat and set aside to cool.

2 Add the cardamom powder and ground peanuts to the syrup. Add half the milk powder, stirring well until blended. Gradually add the remaining milk powder, stirring thoroughly to obtain a smooth and consistent dough. Roll out the dough into small circles and arrange them on a serving dish. Serve with coffee.

 SAUDI ARABIA

MAKES ABOUT 20 ROLLS

For the filling
$10^1/_2$ oz ($1^1/_2$ cups) almonds or walnuts,
  finely ground
1 cup superfine sugar
$1^1/_2$ tsp ground cardamom
A few saffron threads soaked in
  1 tbsp rose water

For the pastry
16–20 sheets filo pastry
1 tbsp cornstarch
8 oz (1 cup) ghee

Nashab
Fried nut rolls

1 Start by making the nut filling. In a bowl, combine all the filling ingredients together.

2 To prepare the pastry, cut the stacked sheets of filo pastry into 4 x 10-inch strips. Cover with a damp towel to keep them from drying out.

3 In a bowl, dissolve the cornstarch in 2 fl oz ($^1/_4$ cup) water. Moisten the edges of the pastry with the cornstarch water, then place 2 tablespoons of nut filling across the narrow end of the pastry strip. Fold the long sides of the pastry over the filling, pressing the folds along each side. Roll up firmly and press the edges to seal securely. Repeat with the remaining quantity.

4 Heat the ghee in a deep pan. Fry about five pastries at a time for 4 minutes, turning the rolls to brown them evenly. When the pastries are a deep golden brown, remove, and drain them on paper towels. Cool before serving. Store at room temperature in an airtight container.

Cream and nut sweets

EGYPT

SERVES 6–8

For the batter
7 tbsp unsalted butter
3/4 cup superfine sugar
1 tsp vanilla extract
2 medium eggs
12 1/2 oz (2 cups) semolina
1 1/2 tsp baking powder
3/4 cup yogurt
2 oz (1/2 cup) blanched almonds

For the sugar syrup
16 fl oz (2 cups) water
2 cups superfine sugar
1 tsp lemon juice

Basbousa
Semolina cake

1 Preheat the oven to 375° F. Start by making the batter. In a large bowl, beat the butter, sugar, and vanilla until light and fluffy. Add the eggs and beat well. Gradually blend in the semolina and the baking powder. Add the yogurt and mix well until the batter is smooth. Spread the batter into a greased 12-inch-round oven-proof pan. Cut into diamond shapes and place an almond in the center of each diamond. Bake for about 35 minutes, until a knife inserted in the center comes out clean.

2 In the meantime, make the sugar syrup: In a saucepan, bring the water and sugar to a boil, then add the lemon juice and reduce the heat. Simmer, uncovered, for 10 minutes, then remove from heat and allow to cool.

3 When the cake is cooked, remove it from the oven and pour the cooled syrup over the hot cake. Cool, cut, and store in an airtight container.

IRAQ

SERVES 4

3 cups water
1/2 cup superfine sugar
1/4 cup (1/2 stick) butter
3 oz (1/2 cup) semolina
1 tbsp rose water
1 tbsp orange-flower water
1/2 tsp ground cinnamon
1 tbsp blanched almonds, to garnish

Mamounia
Semolina pudding

1 To make the sugar syrup, place the water and sugar in a saucepan and bring to a boil. Reduce the heat and simmer for 15 minutes. Set aside.

2 In a separate pan, melt the butter, then add the semolina, stirring constantly for about 5 minutes until golden brown. Stir in the sugar syrup and bring to a boil. Simmer over low heat, stirring constantly until the mixture has thickened. Remove from heat, then add the rose water and orange-flower water.

3 Pour into four serving dishes. Sprinkle with ground cinnamon and garnish with almonds.

Semolina pudding

LEBANON

MAKES 65 PIECES

For the dough
1 lb 2 oz (4¹/2 sticks) butter, softened at
   room temperature
3 cups superfine sugar
4¹/2 cups all-purpose flour, sifted
7 oz (1 cup) pistachios, chopped

For the filling
2 lb 3 oz dates, pitted and minced
3 tbsp butter
¹/4 cup superfine sugar
2 tbsp rose water

Tamara
Shortbread with dates

1 Start by making the dough. Place the butter in a mixing bowl and whisk on full speed with an electric mixer until light and fluffy. Gradually add the sugar, beating until light and creamy. Gradually fold in the flour, whisking the mixture until smooth. Cover the dough and leave to rest in a cool place for 1 hour.

2 To make the filling, combine the dates with the butter, sugar, and rose water.

3 Preheat the oven to 375° F. Divide the dough into walnut-sized pieces. Flatten each piece with your hand and place 1 tablespoon of filling in the center of each piece. Close and form into date shapes. Cover with pistachios. Place on greased baking sheets.

4 Bake for 20 to 25 minutes until very lightly colored. Do not overcook. Leave the shapes on the baking sheets to cool, then remove very carefully and serve or store in an airtight container.

BAHRAIN

SERVES 8

1 lb 2 oz vermicelli
¹/2 cup (1 stick) butter
3 oz (³/4 cup) ground almonds
³/4 cup condensed milk
¹/2 tsp vanilla extract
2 oz (2 cups) corn flakes

Halwa al shairi wal laoz
Almond and vermicelli pastries

1 In a saucepan, fry the vermicelli in the butter until browned. Remove from the butter and drain. Combine the vermicelli with the almonds, condensed milk, vanilla, and half the cereal. Mix well and set aside to cool. Shape the mixture into walnut-sized balls and arrange them on a serving dish. Garnish with the remaining cereal.

Shortbread with dates

SYRIA

MAKES 50 COOKIES

For the sugar syrup
4 fl oz ($^1/_2$ cup) water
1 cup superfine sugar
1 tsp lemon juice
Few drops of rose water or orange-
  flower water

For the dough
9 oz ($2^1/_8$ sticks) butter
$1^1/_2$ cups superfine sugar
$3^3/_8$ cups all-purpose flour
1 tbsp active dry yeast
9 fl oz ($1^1/_8$ cup) milk
9 oz ($2^1/_2$ cups) sesame seeds
1 tbsp butter, melted
$5^1/_2$ oz ($^3/_4$ cup) pistachios, chopped

Barazik

Sesame cookies

1 Start by making the sugar syrup. Place the water and sugar in a small pan and bring to a boil. Simmer for about 10 minutes over moderate heat until the syrup starts to thicken. Add the lemon juice and rose or orange-flower water, then remove from heat and set aside to cool.

2 To make the dough, whisk the unmelted butter with the sugar in a medium bowl until smooth. Stir in the flour, yeast, and milk, beating constantly until smooth. Leave to rest for 15 minutes.

3 Preheat the oven to 375° F. Mix the sesame seeds with the melted butter and sugar syrup. Divide the dough into large walnut-sized balls. Flatten the balls with your fingers into 3-inch circles. Coat one side with the sesame mixture and the other side with the chopped pistachios. Place the cookies onto ungreased baking sheets and bake for 10 minutes until golden brown. Cool and store in an airtight container.

EGYPT

SERVES 6

12¹/₂ oz puff pastry
34 fl oz (4¹/₄ cups) milk
1¹/₄ cups heavy cream
¹/₂ cup superfine sugar
3 oz (¹/₂ cup) raisins
2 oz (¹/₃ cup) pistachios
2 oz (¹/₃ cup) blanched almonds, slivered
2 oz (¹/₃ cup) pine nuts or chopped
   hazelnuts

Um ali

Cream and nut pastry

1 Preheat the oven to 375° F. Roll out the pastry to fit a 12 x 8-inch oven-proof dish. Bake for 10 minutes, until crisp and lightly colored. When cool enough to handle, crush the pastry into medium-sized pieces.

2 Combine the milk, cream, and sugar in a heavy pan and bring to a boil. Reduce the heat and simmer gently for 5 minutes. Leave to cool.

3 In a bowl, mix the pastry pieces with the raisins and nuts. Pour the milk mixture over the pastry mixture and leave to soak for 30 minutes. Bake in the oven for 20 minutes until golden brown. Serve hot.

 IRAN

MAKES 25 PIECES

1 cup superfine sugar
3 tbsp clear runny honey
4 tbsp corn oil
3 oz (³/₄ cup) slivered almonds
¹/₂ tsp ground saffron dissolved in
   2 tbsp rose water
4 tbsp chopped pistachios, to garnish

Shohan asali

Honey almonds

1 Place the sugar, honey, and corn oil in a heavy saucepan. Cook over medium heat, stirring frequently until the sugar is melted and turns golden brown. Add the almonds to the pan and cook for about 2 to 3 minutes, until the almonds are coated.

2 Add the saffron-rose water and cook for 2 minutes, stirring occasionally. Make sure the mixture does not become too dark. Immediately pour teaspoonfuls of the mixture onto an tin-foil-covered baking tray, leaving some space between each. Garnish with chopped pistachios. Allow the honey almonds to cool, then remove and arrange on a serving platter or keep in an airtight container or cookie jar.

SAUDI ARABIA

Muhallabia bil mango

Mango pudding

SERVES 5

For the milk pudding
1^1/8 cups milk
3 tbsp cornstarch
^{1}/3 cup water
^{1}/4 cup superfine sugar
2 tsp rose water

For the mango layer
17 fl oz (2^1/8 cups) mango juice
3 tbsp cornstarch
^{1}/3 cup water
^{1}/4 cup superfine sugar
Whipped cream (optional), to garnish
3 tbsp ground pistachios, to garnish

1 Start by making the milk pudding: Place the milk in a heavy saucepan. In a bowl, dissolve the cornstarch in the water and add to the milk. Bring to a boil, reduce heat and simmer gently for 15 minutes, until the mixture starts to thicken. Add the sugar and rose water and simmer for a further 5 minutes, stirring frequently. Remove from the heat and set aside.

2 To make the mango layer, place the mango juice in a saucepan. In a bowl, dissolve the cornstarch in the water and add to the mango juice. Bring to a boil, reduce heat and simmer gently for 15 minutes, until the mixture starts to thicken. Add the sugar and simmer for 5 more minutes, stirring frequently. Remove from heat.

3 Fill five serving bowls half full with the milk pudding. Top with the mango syrup and garnish with whipped cream, if using, and sprinkle with ground pistachios.

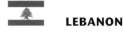 **LEBANON**

MAKES 35–40 CAKES

For the dough
1 lb 10 oz semolina
13 oz (3^1/4 stick) butter
1 tsp active dry yeast
4 tbsp warm water
2 fl oz (^{1}/4 cup) rose water
2 fl oz (^{1}/4 cup) orange-flower water

For the fillings
9 oz (2 cups) coarsely ground walnuts
2 cups superfine sugar
4 tbsp rose water
4 tbsp orange-flower water
9 oz (2 cups) coarsely ground blanched
  almonds
2 decorated molds: 3 inches for the
  almond cakes and 2-inch round for the
  walnut cakes
1 cup confectioners' sugar, to dust

Ma'amoul
Semolina cakes

1 Start by making the dough. Place the semolina in a large bowl. Melt the butter over low heat and pour it over the semolina. Mix until the butter is fully amalgamated. Cover and leave at room temperature overnight.

2 Dissolve the yeast in the warm water, then add it to the semolina mix. In separate pans, heat the rose water and orange-flower water until hot, then pour over the semolina. Mix with your hands to form a smooth dough.

3 Using a food processor, process the semolina mixture in four batches to a malleable dough, then knead the dough lightly with your hands. Place in a bowl, cover with a damp towel and leave to rest for 1 hour at room temperature.

4 To make the walnut filling, mix the walnuts with half the sugar, 2 tablespoons of rose water and 2 tablespoons of orange-flower water. Make the almond filling by mixing the almonds with the remaining sugar, 2 tablespoons of rose water, and 2 tablespoons of orange-flower water.

5 Moisten your hands, then take a piece of dough the size of a large walnut and roll it into a ball. Make a large hole in the ball with your forefinger and squeeze in 2 tablespoons of either nut filling. Close and roll into a ball again.

6 Preheat the oven to 400° F. Press the filled ball into one of the decorated molds, then tap out onto a board. Place the shape on an ungreased baking sheet. Repeat with the remaining balls, using one mold for the walnut-filled pastries and the other for the almond-filled pastries.

7 Bake for 10 minutes until slightly colored. Remove from the oven and leave to cool on the tray for 3 minutes. Very carefully lift the cakes off the tray, taking care not to break them as they will still be soft. Place on trays lined with paper towels. Dust with a generous amount of confectioners' sugar and leave to cool. Store in an airtight container at room temperature.

KUWAIT

Ghraybeh

Shortbread

MAKES 30–35 PIECES

7 oz ($^7/_8$ cup) clarified butter
1 cup superfine sugar
2$^1/_4$ cups all-purpose flour, sifted
2 oz ($^1/_3$ cup) almonds, blanched and peeled

1 Place the clarified butter in a mixing bowl and beat, with an electric mixer on full speed until light and fluffy. Gradually add the sugar, beating until smooth and creamy.

2 Fold in the flour until well blended. Cover the dough and leave to rest in a cool place for 1 hour.

3 Preheat the oven to 300° F. Shape the dough into walnut-sized balls. Place them on ungreased baking sheets. Press the center of each piece gently with your fingers and place an almond in each indentation.

4 Bake for 20 to 25 minutes until very lightly colored. Do not overcook. Leave to cool on the baking trays. Remove very carefully and store in an airtight container.

UNITED ARAB EMIRATES

SERVES 6–8

4 fl oz (^{1}/2 cup) corn oil
6 oz (1 cup) semolina
8 fl oz (1 cup) water
1 lb 9 oz (2 cups) minced dates
1 tsp ground ginger
1 tsp ground cardamom
3 tbsp blanched almonds, to garnish
3 tbsp ground pistachios, to garnish
Confectioners' sugar, to dust

Smid bi tamer

Semolina with dates

1 Heat the corn oil in a pan. Add the semolina and stir until lightly browned. Add the water and stir until all the liquid has been absorbed. Remove from the heat when the semolina starts sticking to bottom of pan. Add the dates, ginger, and cardamom, stirring vigorously until well combined.

2 Pour the date mixture into a large well-greased serving dish and flatten with the back of a spoon. Garnish with the nuts and dust with icing sugar. Cut into squares and serve.

 LEBANON

MAKES TWO 1-QUART JARS

2 lb 3 oz yellow dates
8 cups water
2 oz (^{1}/3 cup) blanched almonds
2^1/2 cups superfine sugar
Peel of 1 mandarin or orange
8 cloves
Juice of ^{1}/2 lemon

Murabba al balah

Preserved dates

1 Wash and peel the dates. Place them in a stainless steel pan, cover with the water, and bring to a boil. Cook over moderate heat for 30 minutes until tender. Remove from the water, drain, and leave to cool in a colander. Reserve the cooking liquid.

2 Remove the pits from the dates, pushing them out with a cocktail stick or a pointed knife. Fill each date with a whole almond. Place the stuffed dates in a stainless steel pan, sprinkle with the sugar, orange peel, cloves, and 1^1/2 cups of the reserved liquid. Soak for 12 hours.

3 Remove the dates from the sugar and water mixture and set aside. Pour the sugar and water into a stainless steel pan, bring to a boil for 5 minutes, skimming any froth as necessary. Add the dates and lemon juice to the pan and simmer for about 20 minutes, until the syrup thickens. Remove from heat and pour into two 1-quart sterilized jars. Leave to cool before tightly closing the jars.

Semolina with dates

Glossary

Bulghur

Cucumber

Dried limes

Freek

Allspice also known as pimento or Jamaican pepper. Available whole or ground. Tastes like a blend of cinnamon, cloves, and nutmeg.

Ashta a thick cream widely used in pastries and sweets. Can be substituted with a mix of $3/4$ ricotta or cottage cheese to $1/4$ whipped heavy cream or mascarpone cheese.

Baharat mixed spices used in the Gulf countries and in Iraq. Baharat can be prepared by mixing the following spices: $1/3$ tsp black pepper, $1/4$ tsp coriander seeds, $1/4$ tsp cinnamon, $1/4$ tsp cloves, $1/3$ tsp ground cumin, 2 tsp cardamom, $1/4$ tsp nutmeg, $1/2$ tsp paprika, $1/4$ tsp dried limes, and $1/4$ tsp curry powder.

Basmati rice a slim and long grain rice with an aromatic flavor. The grains stay firm and separate during cooking. Rinse several times before cooking.

Blanched almonds almonds with skins removed. To blanch almonds, soak them in just-boiled water for 15 minutes. Drain, then press them with your fingers to remove the skins.

Bulghur (cracked wheat) wheat that is hulled, boiled, dried and ground into fine or coarse grains. It is a basic ingredient in Lebanese and Syrian cuisines.

Cardamom available in pods, seeds, or powder. It is preferable to buy the pods because the seeds can be removed and used when needed. It has a distinctive aromatic flavor and is one of the world's most expensive spices.

Chickpeas an irregularly round, sand-colored legume used extensively in Mediterranean cooking. Can be purchased canned or dried.

Chilies come in many types and sizes, both fresh and dried. Use rubber gloves when deseeding and chopping fresh chilies because they can burn the skin. Removing seeds and membranes reduces the heat level.

Cloves dried flower buds of a tropical tree native to Moluccas but also grown in other regions. The buds, stalks, and leaves all yield aromatic oil of clove. Cloves are available whole or ground.

Cilantro *see* Coriander.

Coriander a strongly flavored herb, whose leaves are known as cilantro or Chinese parsley. Its seeds are the main ingredient of curry powder. Cilantro is available fresh and dried, and coriander ground or in seed form. Often stirred into a dish just before serving for maximum impact.

Cucumber the variety used in this book is the long, slender, and thin-skinned Lebanese cucumber, also known as the European or burbles cucumber.

Cumin a spice with a strong and distinctive aroma. Available in seeds or ground.

Dried lime or loomi small, brown or black dried limes. Used frequently in Gulf cooking as well as in Iraq and Iran to impart a lemony flavor. After cooking, remove and discard the limes.

Fava beans used fresh and dried. The fresh bean, when young, has the same shape as green beans and is cooked in the same way. The dried bean is available precooked.

Filo pastry a very thin pastry used for making sweet and savory dishes. Available fresh, chilled, or frozen.

Freek wheat that is picked while still green and then toasted, hulled, and dried.

Ghee (samneh) clarified butter with milk solids removed, so that it will not burn during cooking.

Hamour fish a fat-fleshed grouper fish found in the Gulf region. Can be substituted with cod or rockfish.

Rose buds

Saffron strands

Tamarind

Hawaii can be prepared by mixing the following spices: 3 tsp black pepper, 1$^1/_2$ tsp caraway, $^1/_2$ tsp ground saffron, $^1/_2$ tsp cardamom, 1 tsp turmeric.

Orange-flower water fragrant water extracted by distillation from orange blossoms. It is mainly used in Middle Eastern cuisine to gently flavor sugar syrup and sweets. It is also used as a digestive. Available in Middle Eastern, Greek, and Turkish food shops. Always buy the natural variety.

Parsley parsley used in Middle Eastern cooking is of the flat-leaf variety also known as continental parsley.

Pine nuts also known as pignoli. These small, cream-colored kernels are obtained from the cones of pine trees native to the Mediterranean region. They have a nutty flavor and are commonly used in stuffings and sweets and to garnish meat, chicken, and fish dishes.

Pistachios small, green nuts used unsalted to garnish savory meat and chicken dishes as well as in desserts.

Pita bread or pocket bread most widely used bread in the Middle East. This wheat-flour pocket bread is sold in large, flat pieces that separate easily into two thin circular pieces. Available in supermarkets and in Middle Eastern food stores.

Pomegranate a warm-climate fruit about the size of a large orange, with leathery red skin and a myriad white seeds enveloped in its juicy pink flesh.

Pomegranate molasses reddish-brown sour syrup prepared from sour pomegranate fruit juice.

Purslane a green vegetable with small, fleshy leaves used in salads in the Lebanon and Syria. If unavailable, watercress may be used instead.

Rose water extracted by distillation from a very fragrant pink rose. It is mainly used in Middle Eastern cuisine to flavor some meat dishes, sugar syrup, and in sweets. Always buy the natural variety.

Saffron available in strands or powder. It imparts a yellow-orange color to food once infused. The quality varies greatly; the best is the most expensive spice in the world. If sealed properly, it can be stored in the freezer for up to one year.

Scallion also known as green or spring onion. An immature onion picked before the bulb has fully formed, it has a long, bright green edible stalk and bulb.

Shelled wheat parboiled wheat with the skin or outer membrane removed. Requires little cooking time and is widely available, including at Middle Eastern food stores.

Sumac the dried berries of a shrub that grows wild in the Mediterranean. The berries are ground into a reddish-purple powder. Imparts a sour flavor to salads and other food.

Tahini a thick, buttery fluid made from ground toasted sesame seeds.

Tamarind or Indian date the long, brown pods of a tropical tree with a strongly acidic taste. The dried pods are compressed and packaged like dates. To use, the required quantity is soaked and strained to separate the pulp from the sticky fibers and seeds.

Taro a large, starchy tuber with a dry-textured flesh and a flavor similar to potato. Bitter when eaten raw. Peel before using, but protect hands with rubber gloves because its skin has tiny prickly fibers.

Thyme mix (zaatar) a mix containing dried thyme, sesame seeds, sumac, and salt.

Turmeric a member of the ginger family. Its root is dried and ground, giving a rich yellow powder that is used to color rice, butter, cheese, and mustard. Store in an airtight container.

Vine leaves grapevine leaves are sold canned, fresh, or preserved in brine. If using preserved vine leaves, rinse well to remove the salty flavor, then soak in boiling water for 10 minutes to make pliable. Freeze fresh vine leaves in sealed plastic bags.